The Paschal Mystery

A Primary Source Reader

Lorraine L. Kilmartin

saint mary's press

The publishing team included Gloria Shahin, editorial director; Jeanette Fast Redmond, development editor. Prepress and manufacturing coordinated by the production departments of Saint Mary's Press.

Cover Image @ The Crosiers / Gene Plaisted, OSC

Printed in the United States of America

1360

ISBN 978-1-59982-138-2

Contents

Introduction

The history of salvation stretches all the way back to the beginning of time, and it extends into our lives today and on into the distant future. As that history has unfolded, it has revealed God's eternal Son, Jesus Christ, and the redemption he won for us through his life, Passion, death, Resurrection, and Ascension.

God first created a good world filled with people made in his own divine image. Then sin entered the world, and his plan seemed to be spoiled. But God did not give up so easily. That earth-shaking change in the world and in all of our relationships was followed not by darkness, but by hope. Despite humanity's disobedience, God made many overtures to his beloved people, reaching out again and again through the prophets, offering promises of salvation. Clearly we have a special place in his heart.

The most important figure in salvation history is Jesus, the eternal Son of God, born into human history when the time was right. Jesus came to reveal the living God to humanity. He lived among us and taught us. He suffered and died for our sins. And then he was raised from the dead and ascended into Heaven.

But salvation history does not end there. We take part in it too. God invites us to hope for Heaven and for a better world here on earth because Jesus' saving death has transformed a promise into reality. The Holy Spirit, promised by the Son and sent by his Father, encourages us, strengthens us, and empowers us. The Church continues to teach us what it means to be a follower of Jesus and shows us how God—Father, Son, and Holy Spirit—makes it possible for us to enter into the life of the Holy Trinity through faithful discipleship, Sacraments, and prayer.

The work of salvation accomplished by Jesus Christ—particularly through his Passion, death, Resurrection, and Ascension—is called the Paschal Mystery. This primary source reader explores the Paschal Mystery and all that God has done for us through his Son, Jesus Christ. But the readings here are not like the summaries and explanations of others' ideas you would find in a textbook. Instead each selection expresses its author's own insights. You will read for yourself the words of theologians, poets, Church leaders, and saints. The readings include Bible passages, Church documents, sermons, excerpts from books, essays, even a radio address. Old Testament readings are the oldest selections here, with other selections reflecting our thinking about the Paschal Mystery through the centuries, right up to the twenty-first century.

Some of the selections in this book are easy to follow, telling a story or arguing a viewpoint. Others are more challenging, demanding careful reading—maybe even some rereading. At the end of each chapter, you will find reflection questions to help you think more deeply. Sidebars give more background about related topics and define difficult words too.

Of course, the readings in this book do not form a comprehensive discussion of salvation history. The other materials you use in your course will provide that. Instead this collection of primary sources is intended to provide background about some of the teachings you will study and to answer questions that may come up.

If you read the titles of all six parts in this book, you will find a brief overview of salvation history. Keep that big picture in mind as you read the individual selections. Answers to many questions we have about our faith become clear when we fit them into the context of God's ongoing plan for his beloved people: a plan that ultimately leads to our redemption through our participation in Christ's Paschal Mystery and the life of the Holy Trinity.

Part 1
Our Need for Salvation

1 The Bible: Inspired Text

Introduction

When we want to learn about Jesus and about God's saving work, we turn to the Bible. But how do we know that the Bible is reliable? And how can we be sure that our understanding of its message is correct?

Biblical scholars can help us answer these questions. These men and women have spent a lifetime studying the Bible, most often in the languages in which the texts were first written: Hebrew, Aramaic, and Greek. Although much of their work may be too technical for the ordinary reader, we can gain access to their expertise by consulting a Bible commentary, a book that gathers the writings of respected experts in biblical scholarship. A Bible commentary, as the name implies, provides notes on each passage of the Bible. The observations vary widely, depending on the type of passage being considered. In a Bible commentary, you may read an explanation of some aspect of Hebrew culture, find the history of a biblical idea, or learn that scholars are arguing over how to translate a certain word.

You can also use a Bible commentary to learn more about broader issues in biblical study. Like a theological or biblical dictionary, a commentary may provide background articles on biblical history, literary genres (or types of writing), or important biblical concepts. You will also find an introduction to each book of the Bible, outlining current thinking on the book's specific history, genre, and overall message.

Many Bible commentaries exist, but one of the best known is the *Collegeville Bible Commentary*. It begins with an essay introducing the Bible, written by Dianne Bergant, CSA, a professor of biblical studies at Catholic Theological Union and one of the general editors of the commentary. The introduction discusses big-picture questions that readers may have, such as, How did the Bible develop? What does it mean to say the Scriptures are **inspired**? Why are there so many versions of the Bible? What tools can help us interpret the Bible's teachings?

In the following excerpt, Bergant examines biblical inspiration to address perhaps the most important question: How do we know that the Bible is trustworthy? Bergant explores the mechanism of inspiration—that is, how divine inspiration happens. She then turns her attention to how we can reconcile our belief that the Bible is divinely inspired with the fact that the Bible contains contradictions and scientific errors. Bergant also explains how modern biblical scholars think about this issue.

Second Timothy 3:16 proclaims, "All scripture is inspired by God and is useful for teaching, for refutation, for correction, and for training in righteousness." At the beginning of the excerpt, Bergant affirms Timothy's proclamation, stating that the Bible *was* and *is* inspired.

We can use the approach described in this excerpt to recognize the trustworthiness of the Bible, especially when we encounter narratives that sound like fairy tales to our modern ears. If you keep in mind the distinction between religious truth and scientific or historical truth, as Bergant explains for us here, you will be astounded by the insights you discover when you read the Bible.

inspired Written by human beings with the guidance of the Holy Spirit to teach without error those truths necessary for our salvation.

Excerpt from "Introduction to the Bible," in *The Collegeville Bible Commentary*

By Dianne Bergant, CSA

The Bible *was* inspired, for during its growth and development it continually formed a believing community. The Bible *is* inspired, for it has not ceased to perform this same wonder, giving witness even to this day to the community's origin and continually awakening it to its purpose.

Inspiration and Truth

When one claims that God is the author of the Bible, one is thereby making a statement about its truthfulness. Surely the word of God is trustworthy. God would not deceive the community, nor would God allow the community to be led astray by either the ignorance or the limited perspectives of the human authors. In following this train of thought, many people have insisted that the Bible is inerrant, or free from all error. Such a claim raises several difficult questions.

How does one explain differing and even contradictory traditions? (Human beings were created after the plants and animals appeared—Gen 1:12, 21, 25, 27. Human beings were created while the earth was still uninhabited—Gen 2:5, 9.) Must one adhere to a perception of the universe that is contrary to scientific findings? (Light itself was created before the heavenly bodies that give off light—Gen 1:3, 16.) Can one reconcile conflicting chronology in the Gospel story? (Jesus cleansed the temple at the beginning of his ministry during one of his

> ### Who Wrote the Bible?
>
> Many people ask who wrote the Bible. A better way to phrase the question might be, How did the Bible develop? You may already know that the Bible is actually a collection of texts that many different individuals wrote down over a period of some fifteen hundred years. Much of that content circulated for generations through oral tradition—that is, through storytelling—and those who wrote down the stories sometimes combined different versions of the material to make a unified whole.

several visits to Jerusalem—John 2:13–17. The cleansing occurred during his only visit, which took place just before his death—Matt 21:12–17; Mark 11:15–19; Luke 19:45–48.)

Efforts to explain the inconsistencies found within the Bible have resulted in various methods of interpretation. Those who have opted for **fundamentalist** interpretations have frequently spurned historical and scientific evidence and have adopted the literal sense of the text, claiming that there are no real inconsistencies, for God can do even the impossible if need be.

Another approach attempts to reconcile the theory of inerrancy with the discrepancies present within the text. The Scriptures are taken quite literally until one comes upon a difficult passage. Then, believing that God's **Revelation** can be neither illogical nor inaccurate, the interpreter concludes that what appears to be an inconsistency is really meant to be interpreted allegorically. Thus, what could otherwise be seen as discordant is harmonized.

A third way of resolving the dilemma is to make a decision about the kind of truth the Bible is intended to reveal. Biblical scholars have done just that, distinguishing between historical and/or scientific truth and religious truth—not an easy decision to make. Historical, scientific, and religious references are found to be intertwined. It is not always clear why the authors expressed ideas as they did. If their historical and scientific references are not to be understood as accurate expressions of theological truth, were they merely the best literary and figurative constructions available? Or is the very human, very limited understanding of reality simply the platform from which they launched their profound theological search for God and upon which the drama of God's loving involvement unfolded? However these questions are answered, one must decide which

fundamentalist Based on the literalist meaning of the Bible's words. The interpretation is made without regard to the historical setting in which the writings or teachings were first developed.

Revelation God's self-communication through which he makes known the mystery of his divine plan. Divine Revelation is a gift accomplished by the Father, Son, and Holy Spirit through the words and deeds of salvation history.

guidelines are to be followed when making the distinctions mentioned. Attempting to focus on what in the text is truly theological, critical biblical scholarship has taken great pains to be as honest as possible in applying literary and historical methods of research. In this way it has thrown new light on the question of the truthfulness of the Bible.

At this juncture something should be said about what is meant by "truth." Is it to be understood as something akin to honesty, integrity, the antithesis of deception? Or does it also imply precision, accuracy of fact, freedom from mistake?

Contemporary scholarship insists that the Bible is indeed inspired by God, but inspired through the natural process of the growth and development of tradition. Since the Bible is not merely the record of God's word but also of the human response to that word, the character of human authorship cannot be disregarded. Obvious discrepancies and apparent contradictions may be attributed to human error, but they may also result from those interpretations and reinterpretations produced by the living community over generations of tradition development. Both the needs of a specific community of faith and the particular insights it had into its religious tradition may also have influenced the quality or limitation of theological expression that emerged from the transmission of tradition. One would certainly not reject as either inadequate or in error the theology of Isaiah or Jeremiah simply because the prophets did not refer to or believe in the Trinity or in life after death.

The biblical traditions have been described as testimonies. . . . Those who hold that the words are inspired are more likely to revere the Bible itself as revelation. Others who believe that God is revealed primarily in the events of history are more inclined to regard the Bible as the interpreted testimony to those events. According to this latter view, the Bible is a witness to revelation: the basic difference between these two views, in essence, is the difference between what is said and what is meant. While both perspectives are indeed aspects of the same reality, they most certainly are not identical. Knowing what the Bible says is not the same as knowing what the Bible means.

A study of tradition development indicates that what the community cherished was not primarily some specific expression of the tradition but rather the fundamental meaning of it. Were this not the case, the community consistently would have resisted any attempt at reformulation.

dynamic Marked by continuous change.

As stated earlier, the **dynamic** force operative in the development of the people was God's self-disclosure. The dynamic force operative in the development of the tradition was God's inspiration. The Bible claims to be not only a testimony to God's self-disclosure and to the community's transformation in the past, but also a unique occasion for a comparable disclosure and transformation in the present. To the extent that this claim is verified again and again, the truthfulness of the Bible can be affirmed. It is not so much the accuracy of the words but rather the power of the message that bears witness

> *It is not so much the accuracy of the words but rather the power of the message that bears witness to its truthfulness.*

to its truthfulness. The same Spirit that was operative in the formation of the Scriptures continues to bear witness to its truthfulness and to convince us of its inspired nature. Therein lies the authority of the Bible.

For Reflection

1. Bergant says that "God is the author of the Bible." After reading this chapter, how do you understand this statement?

2. The author mentions three ways of responding to contradictions or inaccuracies in the Bible. Summarize these responses in your own words. In your opinion, which approach seems to have the most benefits or the fewest drawbacks?

3. Bergant asks if truth is parallel to honesty and integrity or if it also implies accuracy of fact. Give an example of a statement that is not factually accurate but still expresses a truth—such as a metaphor or slang expression. What does this exercise help you understand about truth in the Bible?

4. According to Bergant, "It is not so much the accuracy of the words but rather the power of the message that bears witness to its truthfulness." In what ways does the power of the Bible's message make itself known? How does that power demonstrate the Bible's truthfulness?

2 God's Continuous Creation

Introduction

Fr. George Coyne, a Jesuit priest, is the president of the Vatican Observatory Foundation and until 1978 was its director. Coyne has spent his life studying the material that clusters around young stars. In an interview on the PBS documentary *Faith and Reason*, he said that the distribution of this matter "resembles precisely the kind of process that we think took place with the birth of the planets around the sun."

How is it possible for a Jesuit priest and an official of the Vatican to speak so matter-of-factly about the birth of planets? Should he not be telling us that God created the earth in seven days, as Genesis reports? We have all heard about clashes over textbook selection for the science classroom: on one side are Christians who reject evolution in favor of creationism, and on the other side are those who insist that evolution is a scientific fact.

In the article excerpted here, Coyne explains that all areas of human study can contribute to a larger body of knowledge, with different disciplines accepting and substantiating one another's findings. As a Catholic priest and a scientist, he believes it is important to reconcile two realities: theology's teachings about God's role in the universe,

The Pope's Astronomer

Did you know that the Vatican has its own astronomical observatory? It is the oldest astronomical institute in the world, dating back to 1582, when the Vatican assigned scientists and mathematicians to study the consequences of revising the calendar. Today the Vatican Observatory is located not far from Rome at Castel Gandolfo, the papal summer residence, with a second research center in Tucson, Arizona.

and science's teachings about evolution. Coyne has resolved what some see as a contradiction between the Genesis Creation accounts and science by painting a picture of a God who continually creates and nurtures the universe, rather than a God who, at a single fixed moment in time, created the universe as we know it today.

The Catholic Church has always had a high regard for science, while at the same time challenging scientific findings that contradict the revealed truth found in Scripture. As Pope Saint John Paul II said in a 1996 message to the Pontifical Academy of Sciences, apparent contradictions between science and Scripture must be resolved because "truth cannot contradict the truth" (2). But notice that the Pope did not say that we must reject scientific findings that contradict Divine Revelation. In fact, he explained that a rigorous approach to biblical interpretation is necessary to avoid making it "mean something which it is not intended to mean" (3).

In its efforts to understand the origins of humankind, the Church's teaching on evolution has itself evolved over the years. In his 1950 encyclical *Humani Generis,* Pope Pius XII wrote that nothing in Church teaching stood in the way of research into the question of the origins of the human body. He did, however, maintain that human souls "are immediately created by God" (36). Much later, in a 2005 audience, Pope Benedict XVI endorsed the theory of intelligent design, a model that allows for the evolution of species but theorizes that the process itself is directed by God.

Most recently, before a 2009 conference sponsored by the Pontifical Gregorian University in Rome to celebrate the 150th anniversary of Charles Darwin's *On the Origin of the Species,* Archbishop Gianfranco Ravasi, a Vatican official, clarified in an interview that although the Church had been hostile to the theory of evolution in the past, it had never officially condemned the theory. As for intelligent design, news releases about the conference indicated that the topic would be discussed, but only as a "cultural phenomenon," not as a scientific theory (*The Telegraph,* Feb. 11, 2009).

Do these attempts to respond to scientific findings about evolution mean that the Church is confused about its own teaching? Coyne would likely not think so. Instead, he may see in them a sign that the teaching office of the Church is open to integrating findings from other disciplines into her own understanding of the revealed truth of Scripture.

Excerpt from "Can God and Evolution Co-exist? Reflections of a Jesuit Scientist"

By George Coyne, SJ

Evolution as a scientific explanation of origins is often viewed as **atheistic**.

It is not.

Science, by its very methodology, is completely neutral with respect to religious considerations. But if one does believe in God, creator of the universe, can scientific knowledge be helpful in supporting and nurturing that belief?

I would like to discuss how a believing scientist like myself views, based on scientific knowledge, the nature of God and the nature of the human being. Such knowledge is basic to any discussion of faith, and I hope such knowledge complements that derived from philosophy and theology. Several criteria exist to determine the **veracity** of scientific theories, such as predictability, repeatability of experiments, simplicity or economy of explanation. There is, however, a growing awareness among scientists of another criterion: "unifying explanatory power"—not only are the observations at hand explained, but the attempt to understand is also in harmony with all else that we know, even with that which we know outside of the natural sciences. . . .

The **supposition** is that there is a universal basis for our understanding and, since that basis cannot be self-contradictory, the understanding we have from

atheistic Denying the existence of God.

veracity Truthfulness.

supposition An assumption that is taken for granted.

one discipline should complement that which we have from all other disciplines. One is most faithful to one's own discipline, be it the natural sciences, the social sciences, philosophy, literature, religious thought etc., if one accepts this universal basis. This means in practice that, while remaining faithful to the strict truth criteria of one's own discipline, we are open to accept the truth value of the conclusions of other disciplines. And this acceptance must not only be passive, in the sense that we do not deny those conclusions, but also active, in the sense that we integrate those conclusions into the conclusions derived from our own proper discipline.

So, what do we know in this regard from the sciences? It is clear from all of the sciences, including geology, molecular biology, paleontology, comparative anatomy, cosmology and others, that evolution is an intrinsic and proper characteristic of the universe. Neither the universe as a whole nor any of its ingredients can be understood except in terms of evolution. We human beings came to be through evolution, and evolution is a daily happening. As the universe expanded from the Big Bang and evolved, stars were born and stars died. Since stars are born and sustain themselves by creating a thermonuclear furnace whereby light elements are continuously converted into heavier elements, when they die the stars pour out to the universe these heavier elements. And then a second generation of stars is born, not now of pure hydrogen but of the enriched chemistry of the universe. The universe is being continuously enriched with heavier elements. This process continued until, through increasingly complex chemical combinations, the human being came to be. Our sun is a third generation star, and we are literally born of stardust.

This process of being generated by and living with the universe continues every moment of our lives. We are constantly exchanging atoms with the total reservoir of atoms in the universe. Each year 98 percent of the atoms in our bodies are renewed. Each time we breathe we take in billions and billions of atoms recycled by the rest of breathing organisms during the past few weeks. Nothing in my genes was present a year ago. It is all new, regenerated from the available energy and matter in the universe. My skin is renewed each month and my liver each six weeks. Human beings are among the most recycled beings in the universe.

. . . But what relevance does all of this scientific knowledge have to our relationship to God and to faith?

immanence State or quality of being able to be experienced.

The religious believer is tempted by science to make God the "explanation." We bring God in to try to explain things that we cannot otherwise explain. "How did the universe begin?" "How did we come to be?" We latch onto God, especially if we do not feel that we have a good and reasonable scientific explanation. He is brought in as the Great God of the Gaps. I have never come to believe in God by proving God's existence through anything like a scientific process. God is not found as the conclusion of a rational process like that. I believe in God because God gave himself to me. That was not a miracle. It does make sense that there is a personal God who deals with me and loves me and who has given himself to me. I have never come to love God or God to love me because of any of these reasoning processes. I have come to love God because I have accepted the fact that he first made the move towards me. This is what faith is, a personal relationship of love with God, and it must be the source of our pursuit of justice.

Although God transcends the universe, he is working in it through his providence and continuous creation. This stress on God's **immanence** is not to place a limitation upon God. Far from it. It reveals a God who made a universe that has within it, through evolution, a certain dynamism, as seen by science, and thus participates in the very creativity of God. God emptied himself so that he could share his infinite love with his creation. . . .

If they respect the results of modern science, religious believers must move

> *Neither the universe as a whole nor any of its ingredients can be understood except in terms of evolution.*

away from the notion of a dictator God, a Newtonian God who made the universe as a watch that ticks along regularly. Perhaps God should be seen more as a parent or as one who speaks encouraging and sustaining words.

Scripture is very rich in these thoughts. . . . Theologians already possess the concept of God's continuous creation. To explore modern science with this notion of continuous creation and of God's emptying of himself would be an enriching experience for theologians and religious believers.

For Reflection

1. What does Coyne mean when he writes that one measure of accuracy for our knowledge is "unifying explanatory power"?

2. Coyne suggests that constant and ongoing change in the universe allows the universe itself to actively participate in the creativity of God. How can you apply this statement to yourself as a sharer in God's creativity?

3. Coyne writes that God is not found by means of a reasoning process. How does he explain the basis of his own belief in God?

3 Created in the Image of God

Introduction

In the Bible, God clearly expresses his intentions for human beings at the first mention of our creation: "Then God said: 'Let us make human beings in our image, after our likeness'" (Genesis 1:26). Verse 27 explains:

> God created mankind in his image;
> in the image of God he created them;
> male and female he created them.

There is no missing the point: the majestic Creation hymn that forms the opening chapter of the Bible makes it clear that God modeled human beings, male and female, on the Divine. What does it mean to say that we are created in the image of God?

In the first reading in this chapter, from the *United States Catholic Catechism for Adults,* the U.S. bishops describe God's image as a "dynamic source of inner spiritual energy" (p. 67). This energy draws us like a magnet, so that we want to understand and embrace truth and seek to know and love God. When we long for a connection with God, we experience what it means to be created in the image of God.

The *Catechism for Adults* also points to essential human characteristics that result from our creation in the image of God. Notice that each in its own way relates to the concept of harmony or unity. Just as God is a unity of persons in the Blessed Trinity, we who are created in God's image long for harmony in every sphere of life.

In the second reading in this chapter, Barbara A. Kathe, a religious writer and retired professor at Saint Joseph College in

Connecticut, explains, in an article from the journal *Spiritual Life,* her understanding of what it means to be an image of God. Kathe's thinking is related to the ideas in the first reading, though her vocabulary is different. Instead of describing a dynamic force that draws us, she uses a simpler term: *love.* She suggests that one attribute of God is most significant for human beings—God is infinite love. Kathe also reminds us that the human experience of God, as expressed both by the biblical writers and in daily life, is an experience of love and faithfulness. Again and again, through the biblical story of salvation, through the Sacraments of the Church, and through graces we each receive, God reveals himself as steadfast love.

Kathe also explores the more complex concept that God reveals himself as more than a being who loves; God reveals himself as someone who actually is Love. God has revealed that the Holy Trinity is a communion of the three Divine Persons: Father, Son, and Holy Spirit. The relationship that binds them together is love. If God is Love, and we are created in the image of God, then we most clearly reflect that image when we love ourselves, our neighbors, and God. And because being an image of God is not a marginal human quality but rather an essential one, then we are most truly human when we clearly reflect who God is: when we love.

Although the two readings in this chapter offer different perspectives on what it means to be an image of God, both emphasize that being made in his image means that we are always being drawn to share in God's life, and that his life is love.

Excerpt from the *United States Catholic Catechism for Adults*

By the United States Conference of Catholic Bishops

Created in God's Image

> *God willed the diversity of his creatures and their own particular goodness, their interdependence, and their order.*

He destined all material creatures for the good of the human race. Man, and through him all creation, is destined for the glory of God.

—CCC, no. 353

"God created man in his image . . . male and female he created them" (Gn 1:27). In figurative and symbolic language, Scripture describes God's creating the first man and woman, Adam and Eve, and placing them in Paradise. They were created in friendship with God and in harmony with creation. The Church teaches that theirs was a state of original holiness and justice, with no suffering or death (cf. CCC, no. 376; GS, no. 18).

The first man and woman were **qualitatively** different from and superior to all other living creatures on earth. They were uniquely made in the image of God, as are all human beings, their descendants. What does this mean? God's image is not a **static** picture stamped on our souls. God's image is a dynamic source of inner spiritual energy drawing our minds and hearts toward truth and love, and to God himself, the source of all truth and love.

To be made in the image of God includes specific qualities. Each of us is capable of self-knowledge and of entering into communion with other persons through self-giving. These qualities—and the shared heritage of our first parents—also form a basis for a bond of unity among all human beings. To be made in God's image also unites human beings as God's stewards in the care of the earth and of all God's other creatures.

Another important aspect of our creation is that God has made us a unity of body and soul. The human soul is not only the source of physical life for our bodies but is also the core of our spiritual powers of knowing and loving. While our bodies come into being through physical processes, our souls are all created directly by God.

God created man and woman, equal to each other as persons and in dignity. Each is completely human and is meant to complement the other in a communion of persons, seen most evidently in marriage.

qualitatively In a manner related to characteristics or qualities.

static Fixed, motionless.

Finally, we need to recognize that God created the first humans in a state of original holiness and justice, so that we are able to live in harmony with his plan. By his gracious will, he enabled us to know and love him, thus calling us to share his life. Our first parents also had free will and thus could be tempted by created things to turn away from the Creator.

Excerpt from "Image and Likeness"

By Barbara A. Kathe, PhD

Created in the Image of Love

"In the image of himself, in the image of God" (Gen 1:27), we were created. The meaning of that image and likeness is to be found in love, for God is love. . . . We know the power of those things that inhibit our growth in Christ, which transforms us from indifferent and unlovely beings into our true being: love. But we also know that the love of Christ compels us, and it transcends the self-absorbed anguish that blinds us to the Love that gives us life and meaning.

We are not made in the image of the world, but rather through grace we experience an inner drive to discover the image of God in ourselves. Christ encourages and promises us, "Abide in my love. If you keep my commandments, you will abide in my love" (Jn 15:9, 19). If we keep the spirit, as well as the word of the commandments, we will mirror Christ. Jesus makes charity the new commandment. By loving his own "to the end" (Jn 13:1), he makes manifest the Father's love that he receives: "As the Father has loved me, so have I loved you; abide in my love. . . . This is my commandment, that you love one another as I have loved you" (Jn 15:9, 12). Why is it that Christ *commands* us to love as he has loved? It is because love reveals who he is and who we are meant to be.

> 66 *Our loving is a participation in the immensity of the love of the Holy Trinity itself.* 99

Bringing Forth God's Image

Image and likeness: it is a phrase that can be misunderstood. God's likeness is not something that we humans can hear, see, sense, or recreate. What is it then? Essentially, God is God and, as such, necessarily beyond our comprehension. We cannot *know* God and can only describe his attributes **analogically**. We are able to experience God and translate our personal experiences into descriptions that we can comprehend. For us, then, God is infinite Love, Goodness, Wisdom, Power, Mercy—all of these and more. But understandably, the attribute on which we focus most—because we are so often needy and lonely and human—is that of love:

> The God of our faith has revealed himself as He who is; and he has made himself known as "abounding in steadfast love and faithfulness" (Ex 34:6). God's very being is Truth and Love.[1]

It would follow, then, that the reason our true being is revealed when we love is that Christ, who is the image of God's very love for us, brings it forth in us.

Our loving is a participation in the immensity of the love of the Holy Trinity itself, who eternally creates, generates, sustains, and acts in love. But it was only through our redemption by Christ that this participation was won. Each of us has experienced God's love directly through the Redemption, through our individual creation, through Divine mercy, through the Eucharist, and through the graces and mercies we receive every day. Herein lies the mystery of our being, the reason for our existence, and the meaning that sifts through life itself: *The image and likeness of God is Love.*

The image in which we have been cast is Love. Our likeness to God is most vibrant when we are most like God in actions that proceed from love. The very essence of our being is love because Divine Love dwells within us, and we reflect—sometimes radiantly,

analogically Based on an analogy; in this context, the theological principle that even when a comparison can be made between God and humans, God is still more unlike humans than similar to them.

sometimes dimly—that Love which graces us with goodness, humility, and compassion. If we are centered in Christ and respond to the graces that are poured upon us, we will know God as love and we will reach out to others in love. So long as we are self-centered, we will not understand what it means to say that God is love. So long as we are self-centered, we will not be truly human. Our lives will be filled with misplaced ambition, power seeking, and violent or manipulative behavior.

An Insistent Pull to Transformation

Some time ago I met an aged woman, very wise and prayerful. She surprised me one day by revealing her past so that I might understand more fully the limitless boundaries of God's love and mercy. As a young person, Liv had wandered through many dark alleys in life: drugs, alcohol, promiscuity. . . . She was consumed with ambition and, by disregarding the talents and needs of others, she manipulated her way to become the chief operating officer of a large international corporation. Although centered on herself and often ruthless in her actions, she frequently felt a nagging tug toward God. Over the years, this insistent pull became stronger and stronger until she could no longer ignore it. Liv finally began to pray, returned to the sacraments, and discovered God living within her and in others. She spoke to me of God's great patience, forgiveness, and mercy, and rejoiced in his love for her. She had found that Love "binds everything together in perfect harmony" (Col 3: 14). Today . . . her experience of God's love remains intense, personal, and far reaching. Despite her now frail and aged body, she is radiantly alive, loving and kind, clearly empowered as a channel of grace for others by the Love in which her life is now centered.

The Bathroom Mirror

You cannot see your own image in the bathroom mirror after a hot shower, when the mirror is fogged up. Once the surface has been cleaned off, your image is again reflected in the mirror. The Creation narrative in Genesis tells us that we are images of God. That is our essential nature, what we are, at heart. But like a fogged-up mirror that cannot reflect our image, we do not always reflect God's image as he intended. God's promise of salvation is a promise to fully restore his image in us.

Like Liv, each of us is offered graces for our own renewal and transformation. The real transformation, the true image that we seek, is the one in which we were created. It is through the discovery of God's image within us that change begins. Christ shows us how to share his humanity by choosing works of humility, love, compassion, and truth. Christ taught, healed, comforted, and sought justice. . . .

Christ's teachings outline a way of life that is permeated with love, both love of God and love of neighbor. Only by loving can we imitate Christ. When we love, God abides in us. When we love, God enlightens us. When we love, God strengthens us. Openness to grace for even the first effort to be poor in spirit, just, merciful, a peacemaker or to practice justice, or any of the beatitudes leads to a fuller understanding of Christ, and a deeper relationship with him and with others.

Endnote

1. *Catechism*, Pt. 1, Art. 231.

For Reflection

1. The first reading, from the *Catechism for Adults*, identifies several human characteristics associated with being created as images of God. In your own words, summarize these characteristics. Which one are you most aware of in your own life?

2. According to the second reading, in what ways does God continually show love for humanity?

3. What did Liv, the prayerful woman who revealed her past to Kathe, discover late in life? How did this discovery change her?

4. At the end of her reading, Kathe lists graces that can come to people who love. Which of these gifts would you most like to receive from God? Why?

4 Original Sin: The Human Condition

Introduction

One way to think about Original Sin is to recognize it as part of the universal human experience. Have you ever felt caught in a struggle between good and evil as you faced a personal decision? Have you found yourself doing something that you swore you would never do again? Have you wondered why your conscience does not jump in to prevent you from doing something wrong before it is too late? Welcome to the human race! These experiences are among the effects of Original Sin described in the three excerpts here.

The first excerpt is from Saint Paul's Letter to the Romans. In one of the best New Testament descriptions of the effects of Original Sin, this saintly leader of the early Church—a man who heard the Risen Christ address him personally—expresses his disgust with his own behavior: "I do not do what I want, but I do what I hate" (Romans 7:15). Every person on earth can say the same about himself or herself at times. The excerpt ends with a rhetorical question: Who will save me? Paul, of course, knows the answer—an answer he shared with anyone, anywhere in the Roman world, who would listen to his preaching about the Risen Christ.

The topic of Original Sin is also the subject of the second reading, from one of the documents of the **Second Vatican Council**, the *Pastoral Constitution on the Church in the Modern World*—also known by its Latin name, *Gaudium et Spes*. In this excerpt the Council restates the teaching that humanity (referred to as "man" in some Church documents) was originally holy and did not experience the effects of evil and sin as we do today. The Council affirms what the Book of Genesis relates: when God created man, male and female, he saw that they were good, just like all of creation. But our first ancestors, as that biblical narrative tells us, allowed themselves to be seduced by evil. The excerpt goes on to explain how Original Sin touches our daily lives, and it assures us that God offers release from the bondage of sin through Jesus.

The last excerpt in this chapter is a devotional reflection from John Donne, the great metaphysical English poet who wrote during the late sixteenth and early seventeenth centuries—around the same time as Shakespeare. Donne offers a vivid metaphor for Original Sin, an image that will be familiar to anyone who has ever built a fire. God, he says, placed a glowing coal of immortality in our hearts—but instead of breathing gently on it to coax it into flame, we blew it out. Donne recognizes that God has given each of us a conscience to help us avoid sin, but he wonders why we do not listen to our conscience. Because Donne was writing in Elizabethan times, his language can seem archaic, but read carefully to get the full impact of his humorous exaggeration as he describes our "miserable condition." Like Saint Paul, Donne acknowledges that it is Jesus who ultimately will save us from our misery.

As bleak as these descriptions of the human condition may be, each contains the seeds of hope. The state of Original Sin is a universal human condition that involves struggle—but as we become more aware of that struggle, these readings point out, we also become more aware of our need for God.

> **Second Vatican Council**
>
> Vatican II was the ecumenical or general Council of the Roman Catholic Church that Pope Saint John XXIII convened in 1962. It continued under Pope Paul VI until 1965. Among the many issues it addressed, the Council clarified the role of the Church in the world, called for a revision of the liturgy, and revived the central role of Scripture in the life of the Church. Few areas of Church life remained the same after Vatican Council II.

Romans 7:15–24

What I do, I do not understand. For I do not do what I want, but I do what I hate. Now if I do what I do not want, I concur that the law is good. So now it is no longer I who do it, but sin that dwells in me. For I know that good does not dwell in me, that is, in my flesh. The willing is ready at hand, but doing the good is not. For I do not do the good I want, but I do the evil I do not want. Now if [I] do what I do not want, it is no longer I who do it, but sin that dwells in me. So, then, I discover

> 66 *I do not do what I want, but I do what I hate.* 99

the principle that when I want to do right, evil is at hand. For I take delight in the law of God, in my inner self, but I see in my members another principle at war with the law of my mind, taking me captive to the law of sin that dwells in my members. Miserable one that I am! Who will deliver me from this mortal body?

Excerpt from *Pastoral Constitution on the Church in the Modern World (Gaudium et Spes)*

By the Second Vatican Council

13. Although he was made by God in a state of holiness, from the very onset of his history man abused his liberty, at the urging of the Evil One. Man set himself against God and sought to attain his goal apart from God. Although they knew God, they did not glorify Him as God, but their senseless minds were darkened and they served the creature rather than the Creator (cf. *Rom.* 1:21–25). What divine revelation makes known to us agrees with experience. Examining his heart, man finds that he has inclinations toward evil too, and is engulfed by manifold ills which cannot come from his good Creator. Often refusing to acknowledge God as his beginning, man has disrupted also his proper relationship to his own ultimate goal as well as his whole relationship toward himself and others and all created things.

Therefore man is split within himself. As a result, all of human life, whether individual or collective, shows itself to be a dramatic struggle between good and evil, between light and darkness. Indeed, man finds that by himself he is incapable of battling the assaults of evil successfully, so that everyone feels as though he is bound by chains. But the Lord Himself came to free and strengthen man, renewing him inwardly and casting out that "prince of this world" (*John* 12:31) who held him in the bondage of sin (cf. *John* 8:34). For sin has diminished man, blocking his path to fulfillment.

The call to grandeur and the depths of misery, both of which are a part of human experience, find their ultimate and simultaneous explanation in the light of this revelation.

Excerpt from Devotion I, *"Insultus morbi primus"* [The First Alteration, the First Grudging, of the Sickness], in *Devotions Upon Emergent Occasions*
By John Donne

Meditation

. . . O miserable condition of man! which was not imprinted by God, who, as he is immortal himself, had put a coal, a beam of immortality into us, which we might have blown into a flame, but blew it out by our first sin; we beggared ourselves by hearkening after false riches, and infatuated ourselves by hearkening after false knowledge. . . .

Expostulation

. . . My God, my God, why is not my soul as **sensible** as my body? Why hath not my soul these apprehensions, these **presages**, these changes, these **antidates**,

sensible In this context, having the ability to perceive or detect something.

presages Predictions or foreknowledge.

antidates Anticipations about the future; literally, "dates before dates."

importune To beg or pester someone for something.

these jealousies, these suspicions of a sin, as well as my body of a sickness? Why is there not always a pulse in my soul to beat at the approach of a temptation to sin? . . . I stand in the way of temptations, naturally, necessarily; all men do so; for there is a snake in every path, temptations in every vocation; but I go, I run, I fly into the ways of temptation which I might shun; nay, I break into houses where the plague is, I press into places of temptation, and tempt the devil himself, and solicit and **importune** them who had rather be left unsolicited by me. I fall sick of sin, and am bedded and bedrid, buried and putrified in the practice of sin, and all this while have no presage, no pulse, no sense of my sickness. . . . Thou hast imprinted a pulse in our soul, but we do not examine it; a voice in our conscience, but we do not hearken unto it. We talk it out, we jest it out, we drink it out, we sleep it out; and when we wake, we do not say with Jacob, *Surely the Lord is in this place, and I knew it not:* but though we might know it, we do not, we will not. But will God pretend to make a watch, and leave out the spring? to make so many various wheels in the faculties of the soul, and in the organs of the body, and leave out grace, that should move them? or will God make a spring, and not wind it up? . . . we have received our portion, and misspent it, not been denied it. We are God's tenants here, and yet here, he, our landlord, pays us rents; not yearly, nor quarterly, but hourly, and quarterly; every minute he renews his mercy. . . .

Prayer

. . . Thy voice received in the beginning of a sickness, of a sin, is true health. If I can see that light betimes, and hear that voice early, *Then shall my light break forth as the morning, and my health shall spring forth speedily* (Isaiah 58:8). . . . O my God . . . keep me still established, both in a constant assurance, that thou wilt speak to me at the beginning of every such sickness, at the approach of every such sin; and that, if I take knowledge of that voice then, and fly to thee, thou wilt preserve me from falling, or raise me again, when by natural infirmity I am fallen. Do this,

O Lord, for his sake, who knows our natural infirmities, for he had them, and knows the weight of our sins, for he paid a dear price for them, thy Son, our Saviour, Christ Jesus. Amen.

For Reflection

1. What do the readings mean when they suggest that sin is a kind of slavery or bondage?

2. Each reading uses images or physical representations to describe our human struggle with sin. Summarize some of the images. Which speaks most clearly to you, and why?

3. The reading from the Second Vatican Council and the devotion by John Donne both refer to God's role in our struggle with sin. How do they say God helps us?

Part 2
Christ: A Promise Fulfilled

5 God's Unbroken Promises

Introduction

You may know that the term *Old Testament,* referring to the first part of the Bible, literally means "Old Covenant." But do not be fooled into thinking that *old* means *outdated.* The term refers to covenants God made with the Hebrew people, covenants pre-dating the New Covenant, which was sealed with Jesus' blood. In these earlier, everlasting covenants, God promised again and again, "You will be my people, and I will be your God" (Ezekiel 36:28). God's promise does not mean merely "You will worship me; I will be the god you worship." When God says, "I will be your God," he implies much more.

Perhaps your mother has said to you, "No matter how old you are, you'll always be my child." Or maybe a childhood buddy once promised to be your friend forever. You may have attended a wedding where the bride and groom promised to be husband and wife for the rest of their lives. As we reflect on the commitment contained in these promises, we begin to understand the concept of covenant. Of course, some mothers do abandon their children, many childhood friends do part, and not all marriages last until the death of one spouse. But God's eternal promises are never broken.

This chapter provides excerpts from four books of the Old Testament—Sirach, Psalms, Isaiah, and Ezekiel. These passages highlight the many covenants God made with his people before the time of Jesus. These covenants were not abandoned; on the contrary, they were fulfilled in the coming of Jesus.

The first reading, from Sirach, tells about the covenant God made with Noah, who acted on behalf of all created beings; in this

38

covenant God promised never again to destroy all living things. The Sirach passage next mentions the covenants made with Abraham, Isaac, and Jacob, promising that God's People will be a great nation with a land of its own. The sign of this ancient covenant, which was carried forward through Abraham's son Isaac and his grandson Jacob, is **circumcision**, a practice observed throughout history as a symbol of Jewish identity as God's Chosen People. Those with faith in Jesus are added to this community of Abraham's faithful descendents, as we know from the Letter to the Romans in the New Testament. In that letter Paul compares believers who are not of Jewish descent to branches that are grafted onto an olive tree: they are able to share in the root of the tree and be nourished by it (Romans 11:1–24).

In the passage given here, Sirach goes on to name the covenant with Moses, the great leader who received the Ten Commandments on behalf of the people. This covenant requires God's people to obey the laws revealed at Mount Sinai. The first three commandments ensure fidelity to God, and the remaining seven require community members to respect one another. Recall that Jesus, in his Sermon on the Mount, assures his listeners that this Sinai Covenant is indeed an everlasting bond: "Do not think that I have come to abolish the law or the prophets. I have come not to abolish but to fulfill" (Matthew 5:17).

In the second passage in this chapter, Psalm 89, we read about God's promise to David, the great king: God will never abandon him, and his dynasty will be everlasting. We know that Jesus continues that dynasty; the narrative of Jesus' birth in the Gospel of Matthew names David as an ancestor of Jesus (Matthew 1:6). God's promise to the warrior-king of the Old Testament is fulfilled in Jesus, the savior-king of the New Testament.

The third excerpt, from Isaiah, paints a picture of a loving and generous God who offers abundance, as well

circumcision The act, required by Jewish Law, of removing the foreskin of the penis. It has been a sign of God's Covenant relationship with the Jewish people.

Food for the Hungry Soul

Shortly after Jesus feeds a crowd of thousands who have gathered to hear him by multiplying five loaves and two fishes, he tells the people, "I am the bread of life; whoever comes to me will never hunger, and whoever believes in me will never thirst" (John 6:35). In word and deed, Jesus demonstrates that the Father honors his promises of abundance. God continues to honor those promises today, feeding all who seek him in the Holy Eucharist.

as forgiveness, to his people. These gifts are likewise fulfilled in Jesus. Recall that the Gospel of John, for example, calls Jesus "the bread of life" (John 6:35) as well as "the Lamb of God, who takes away the sin of the world" (1:29).

In the last excerpt, Ezekiel relays God's promise to forgive the Hebrew people, even though they have repeatedly turned away from God to worship idols. This passage explains God's plan for the Hebrew people: they are to reveal his saving power to the world: "I will show the holiness of my great name. . . . Then the nations shall know that I am the Lord" (Ezekiel 36:23). God promises to give his people a new heart and to place his own spirit within them. The actions of the Risen Christ, described in the Gospel of John, echo this promise. Appearing among them after the Resurrection, Jesus breathes on the Apostles, saying, "Receive the holy Spirit" (John 20:22).

Just as God's promises gave hope to the Hebrew people, they can comfort us today. They remind us that God keeps his promises and is always with us. Even in those moments when life appears to stretch bleakly before us, with no hope in sight, we can find comfort in turning to God's remarkable promises. The beautiful language with which these excerpts express God's deep, providential care can soothe the troubled soul. Promises alone cannot heal us. But knowing that all of God's promises are fulfilled in Jesus? That is truly food for the soul.

NOAH, found just and perfect,
> renewed the race in the time of devastation.

Because of his worth there were survivors,
> and with a sign to him the deluge ended.

A lasting covenant was made with him,
> that never again would all flesh be destroyed.

ABRAHAM, father of many peoples,
> kept his glory without stain:

He observed the Most High's command,
> and entered into a covenant with him;

In his own flesh he incised the ordinance,
> and when tested was found loyal.

For this reason, God promised him with an oath
> to bless the nations through his descendants,

To make him numerous as grains of dust,
> and to exalt his posterity like the stars,

Giving them an inheritance from sea to sea,
> and from the River to the ends of the earth.

For ISAAC, too, he renewed the same promise
> because of Abraham, his father.

The covenant with all his forebears was confirmed,
> and the blessing rested upon the head of ISRAEL.

God acknowledged him as the firstborn,
> and gave him his inheritance.

He fixed the boundaries for his tribes
> and their division into twelve.

From him came the man
> who would win the favor of all the living:

Dear to God and human beings,
> MOSES, whose memory is a blessing.

God made him like the angels in honor,
> and strengthened him with fearful powers.

At his words God performed signs
> and sustained him in the king's presence.

He gave him the commandments for his people
and revealed to him his glory.

Psalm 89:19–38

Truly the LORD is our shield,
the Holy One of Israel, our king!
Then you spoke in vision;
to your faithful ones you said:
"I have set a leader over the warriors;
I have raised up a chosen one from the people.
I have chosen David, my servant;
with my holy oil I have **anointed** him.
My hand will be with him;
my arm will make him strong.
No enemy shall outwit him,
nor shall the wicked defeat him.
I will crush his foes before him,
strike down those who hate him.
My faithfulness and mercy will be with him;
through my name his horn will be exalted.
I will set his hand upon the sea,
his right hand upon the rivers.
He shall cry to me, 'You are my father,
my God, the Rock of my salvation!'
I myself make him the firstborn,
Most High over the kings of the earth.

> **anointed** Having oil poured over one's head. In Old Testament practice, those chosen by God for a special role were anointed as a sign that God's spirit had come upon them.

Forever I will maintain my mercy for him;
my covenant with him stands firm.
I will establish his dynasty forever,
his throne as the days of the heavens.
If his descendants forsake my teaching,
do not follow my decrees,
If they fail to observe my statutes,
do not keep my commandments,

I will punish their crime with a rod
and their guilt with blows.
But I will not take my mercy from him,
nor will I betray my bond of faithfulness.
I will not violate my covenant;
the promise of my lips I will not alter.
By my holiness I swore once for all:
I will never be false to David.
His dynasty will continue forever,
his throne, like the sun before me.
Like the moon it will stand eternal,
forever firm like the sky!"

Isaiah 55:1–11

All you who are thirsty,
come to the water!
You who have no money,
come, buy grain and eat;
Come, buy grain without money,
wine and milk without cost!
Why spend your money for what is not bread;
your wages for what does not satisfy?
Only listen to me, and you shall eat well,
you shall delight in rich fare.
Pay attention and come to me;
listen, that you may have life.
I will make with you an everlasting covenant,
the steadfast loyalty promised to David.
As I made him a witness to peoples,
a leader and commander of peoples,
So shall you summon a nation you knew not,
and a nation that knew you not shall run to you,
Because of the LORD, your God,
the Holy One of Israel, who has glorified you.

Seek the LORD while he may be found,
  call upon him while he is near.
Let the wicked forsake their way,
  and sinners their thoughts;
Let them turn to the LORD to find mercy;
  to our God, who is generous in forgiving.
For my thoughts are not your thoughts,
  nor are your ways my ways—oracle of the LORD.
For as the heavens are higher than the earth,
  so are my ways higher than your ways,
  my thoughts higher than your thoughts.
Yet just as from the heavens
  the rain and snow come down
And do not return there
  till they have watered the earth,
  making it fertile and fruitful,
Giving seed to the one who sows
  and bread to the one who eats,
So shall my word be
  that goes forth from my mouth;
It shall not return to me empty,
  but shall do what pleases me,
  achieving the end for which I sent it.

Ezekiel 36:16–17,18–28

The word of the LORD came to me: Son of man, when the house of
Israel lived in its land, they defiled it with their behavior and their
deeds. . . . So I poured out my fury upon them for the blood they
poured out on the ground and for the idols with which they defiled it. I
scattered them among the nations, and they were dispersed through other
lands; according to their behavior and their deeds I carried out judgment
against them. But when they came to the nations, where they went, they
desecrated my holy name, for people said of them: "These are the people

of the Lord, yet they had to leave their land." So I relented because of my holy name which the house of Israel desecrated among the nations to which they came. Therefore say to the house of Israel: Thus says the Lord God: Not for your sake do I act, house of Israel, but for the sake of my holy name, which you desecrated among the nations to which you came. But I will show the holiness of my great name, desecrated among the nations, in whose midst you desecrated it.

> 66 *You will be my people, and I will be your God.* 99

Then the nations shall know that I am the Lord—oracle of the Lord God—when through you I show my holiness before their very eyes. I will take you away from among the nations, gather you from all the lands, and bring you back to your own soil. I will sprinkle clean water over you to make you clean; from all your impurities and from all your idols I will cleanse you. I will give you a new heart, and a new spirit I will put within you. I will remove the heart of stone from your flesh and give you a heart of flesh. I will put my spirit within you so that you walk in my statutes, observe my ordinances, and keep them. You will live in the land I gave to your ancestors; you will be my people, and I will be your God.

For Reflection

1. Sirach 44:20 refers to a test of Abraham's faith. What Old Testament narrative does Sirach call to mind?

2. According to Psalm 89, how will God treat those who are unfaithful to him?

3. How can we interpret the last two verses of the excerpt from Isaiah, in light of the term used for Jesus in the Gospel of John, *the Word*?

4. In Ezekiel God says, "I will give you a new heart, and a new spirit I will put within you" (36:26). How do you understand the need for a new heart and spirit? What would these gifts mean for you?

6 The Ancient Prophecies Fulfilled

Introduction

Old Testament prophecies promise deliverance and salvation, a time when God will reign. Have these prophecies come true yet? Yes and no. During the season of Advent, the time of preparation before Christmas, the Church looks forward to the "yes": Christ the Savior is born. At the same time, the Church is aware of the "no," better stated as "not fully." The birth of Jesus ushered in the Reign of God, but we still look forward to the day when the Old Testament promises will be fully realized.

Mary looked forward to that day too and seemed to be aware of the tension between "here now" and "not fully present." In the Gospel of Luke, when Mary learns that she is to be the mother of the Savior, she proclaims the song (or canticle) of praise that we know today as the *Magnificat* (Luke 1:46–55)—the first reading in this chapter. Mary sings the praises of God not only because he has done great things for her personally but also because he has brought justice to the world. God has taken rulers from their thrones, provided for those who are hungry, and saved Israel. But Mary seems to be singing about things that are yet to come. The seeds of these events will grow along with the child in her womb, but they will not come to full fruition even during that child's lifetime. The promise of the *Magnificat* reaches forward to the future but also reaches back into time. It recalls the promises God made to his people, promises that we find in the Old Testament.

These same promises are the focus of special Advent prayers called the O Antiphons, given here as the second reading. These **antiphons** remind us of the Old Testament's promise of the arrival of a Savior, Jesus Christ, the Word Incarnate. The O Antiphons use a different title for Christ each day, such as Wisdom, Key of David, and Emmanuel. These titles come from prophecies about the Messiah found in the Book of Isaiah. We hear the O Antiphons in the Alleluia verses during daily Masses in the last week before Christmas. Catholics who pray the Divine Office during this week also chant or recite one of the O Antiphons during each Evening Prayer, commonly known as Vespers, before praying the *Magnificat*. The *Magnificat* is always part of Evening Prayer; but like the prophecies of Isaiah, it takes on

The Divine Office

The Divine Office, or Liturgy of the Hours, is a structured form of prayer, designating certain times for prayer throughout the day. The practice of praying around the clock developed in medieval monasteries in response to Christ's directive to "pray always" (Luke 18:1). Every day, all over the world, many Catholics organize their day around Morning and Evening Prayer. The Divine Office ensures that the day is anchored to God's Word and establishes a connection to the universal Church.

special significance during Advent, when we again await the birth of our Savior.

By directing our attention to the Old Testament prophecies about the promised Messiah, the O Antiphons remind us that God's People have long been waiting for the birth of the Messiah, well before our own waiting begins anew each Advent. Isaiah prophesied that the Spirit of the Lord, with the attendant gift of wisdom, would rest on the One who was to come. Although Isaiah never expected that the Messiah would be God Made Flesh, he knew that the Lord would offer salvation. Saying that the Messiah would be a descendent of Jesse and his son King David, Isaiah predicted that the Messiah would possess the key to David's house, throne, and kingdom. Isaiah foretold that the Messiah would bring light to a dark world, that he would judge the nations, and that he would be called Emmanuel,

antiphons Short statements, often set to music, that come before or after a psalm or other biblical prayer.

A Hidden Promise

The medieval monks who wrote the O Antiphons might have left a clue for us in the intricate theological language. If we look at the Latin text and take the first letter of each invocation in order—Sapientia, Adonai, Radix, Clavis, Oriens, Rex, Emmanuel—we get the letters SARCORE. When read backward, the letters spell the Latin sentence *Ero cras*, an Advent promise: "I come tomorrow." The O Antiphons offer a promise that is hidden, just as the Christ child is hidden in Mary's womb during Advent.

which means God-with-us. All of these prophecies formed the starting point for the O Antiphons.

In this chapter's third excerpt, from *Seven Bells to Bethlehem: The O Antiphons*, Oliver Treanor explores practices and meanings associated with the O Antiphons. He describes the customs that medieval monasteries observed regarding the O Antiphons, which may have been composed as early as the sixth century. He explains that those last days before Christmas commemorate the days when Mary, the expectant mother, was traveling toward Bethlehem, where her arrival culminated in the birth of the Christ child. Treanor explains that the "O" of the antiphons came to be associated with the round shape of the expectant Mother of God. He reflects on the similarities between Mary as mother-to-be and the Church. Both are awaiting the coming of Christ, and both are "heavy with salvation," in his words—they share the mission of bringing Christ into the world.

Treanor points out that during Advent the Church waits in two ways. In the first sense, which is liturgical, Christ does come to us at the end of our Advent waiting, when we celebrate and remember his birth at Christmas. But in a second sense, we are still waiting, because we will not experience the fullness of Christ's coming until he comes in glory at the end of time.

All of the readings in this chapter draw a line from God's promises in the Old Testament to the saving work of Jesus Christ in the New Testament. Looking back at those promises over time and recognizing that Jesus came to fulfill them allows us to look forward in hope to the day when God's promises will be fully realized.

The *Magnificat* (Luke 1:46–55)

And Mary said:
"My soul proclaims the greatness of the Lord;
    my spirit rejoices in God my savior.
For he has looked upon his handmaid's lowliness;
    behold, from now on will all ages call me blessed.
The Mighty One has done great things for me,
    and holy is his name.
His mercy is from age to age
    to those who fear him.
He has shown might with his arm,
    dispersed the arrogant of mind and heart.
He has thrown down the rulers from their thrones
    but lifted up the lowly.
The hungry he has filled with good things;
    the rich he has sent away empty.
He has helped Israel his servant,
    remembering his mercy,
according to his promise to our fathers,
    to Abraham and to his descendants forever."

The O Antiphons from the *Lectionary for Mass*

December 17

O Wisdom of our God Most High,
guiding creation with power and love:
come to teach us the path of knowledge!

December 18

O Leader of the House of Israel,
giver of the Law to Moses on Sinai:
come to rescue us with your mighty power!

December 19

> O Root of Jesse's stem,
> sign of God's love for all his people:
> come to save us without delay!

December 20

> O Key of David,
> opening the gates of God's eternal Kingdom:
> come and free the prisoners of darkness!

December 21

> O Radiant Dawn,
> splendor of eternal light, sun of justice:
> come and shine on those who dwell in darkness and in the shadow
> of death!

December 22

> O King of all nations and keystone of the Church:
> come and save man, whom you formed from the dust!

December 23

> O Emmanuel, our King, and Giver of Law:
> come to save us, Lord our God!

Excerpt from *Seven Bells to Bethlehem: The O Antiphons*

By Oliver Treanor

Foreword

It was the custom in the Middle Ages throughout the monasteries of Europe to sing the O antiphons with the Magnificat at Vespers in the week leading up to Christmas. Each evening from December 17 to 23, the antiphon proper to the Office was intoned by a different monk in descending rank order, beginning with the Abbot.

During the singing of the Canticle and its antiphon the largest bell in the community was rung from the **campanile**. Like the Angelus bell today which calls to mind the incarnation, it called the faithful to rejoice as it marked off the days approaching the Nativity. Wherever its sonorous tone was heard—over high slopes in Germany or France, along upper Alpine valleys, across Swiss mountain cantons or down on the flood plains of Italy—it invited men to join with the spirit of Mary on her journey to Bethlehem, and to share with her, through repentance and prayer, the grace of giving birth to the Saviour.

Though far from Palestine, the sound of the seven bells brought Bethlehem close to the hearts and minds of Christians everywhere, but to none more than those who chanted the antiphons and pondered deeply on their meaning.

Introduction: The Great "O" of Advent

. . . The "O" antiphons are the distinctive prayers of Advent. They hallow the time of preparation for Christ's birth. That this is the case is partly because they belong to the liturgy—the Divine Office which sanctifies the Hours, and the Eucharist which centres and completes the consecration of the day to the Lord, and partly because they are themselves a rich source of meditation on Advent and on the One whose coming is ardently awaited. . . .

The very shape of the "O" which gives them their name conveys this [completion]. It is a figure of fullness. A kind of hieroglyph of that text in St. Paul which puts into words what the symbolic "O" signifies. "When the time had fully come, God sent forth his Son, born of a woman . . . so that we might receive adoption as sons" (Gal. 4:4–5). The yearly round of Advent recalls the perfection of God's timing in the mystery of redemption. It makes that moment present again through thankful remembrance. But more than this, it proclaims that Time itself is fulfilled, being now filled with the fullness of him in whom dwells the fullness of God. . . .

Since the Great "O" suggests ripe fullness, it images the womb of the

> **campanile** Bell tower, often built alongside a church or monastery or as part of them, especially in medieval architecture.

Virgin in late pregnancy, round and full of Christ. From the period when the "O" antiphons were first sung in the monasteries of Europe, Mary was known as the "O" Madonna. Medieval frescoes depict the Virgin of Advent large and maternal, venerable through Christ-bearing. The 'O' also reflects the catholicity of the Church, full of the grace of Christ's indwelling in ministry, sacrament, holy scripture and two thousand years of worship. Mary's other title in the Middle Ages was Mother of the Church. Contemporary painting showed her . . . sheltering the children of God in her all-encompassing mantle. Thus up to the fourteenth century, art and the antiphons envisaged Mary and the Church as typified equally by the "O," sharing the same function that the "O" represented, of carrying Christ to the world. . . .

> 66 **The Great "O" then ultimately stands for Mary and the Universal Church, both expectant of the Messiah.** 99

The Great "O" then ultimately stands for Mary and the Universal Church . . . both expectant of the Messiah. One as Mother of the historical Jesus, Head of the Body; the other as Community of **eschatological** hope in which are born the members of that Body. Each heavy with salvation. Each announcing with perfect conviction the certainty of his coming. . . .

eschatological Having to do with the last things: the Last Judgment, the particular judgment, the resurrection of the body, Heaven, Hell, and Purgatory.

Adonai Hebrew word meaning "Lord" or "Leader," traditionally uttered instead of the actual name of God, Yahweh, which observant Jews do not speak aloud.

vocative A grammatical term meaning that a word directly addresses the reader or listener.

The invocations call on the Child of Mary's womb with names that are full of faith. As Mary herself undoubtedly did in those last few days of tender contemplation before his birth. O Wisdom! O **Adonai**! O Root of Jesse! O Key of David! O Rising Sun! O Desire of Nations! O Emmanuel! Here is a Child that is deeply desired: on him rests the fate of a people broken by sin, a people as good as dead until brought to second birth. Thus the capital "O" is first of all a **vocative** "O." It addresses each title to the Messiah personally, though he be invisible. Invisible, but not absent. While hidden in the depths of his Mother, he is as present as in the baptized soul of every Christian. His glory too is there. Though eclipsed by his infancy, it is as real as its own reflection in the womb of every heart that longs for him. Thus the tension is maintained and respected: weak he may be in his nameless embryonic state, but by his titles of honour he brings a power that will save.

This is why the "O" is repeated at the end of the antiphon—this time as an urgent supplication. "O come and teach us," "O come and save," "O come to deliver us," "O come to free the captive," "O come and enlighten us," "O come and save man," "O come and save us." We who make these appeals may well be redeemed, but we labour under the shadow of original sin. Until he comes to be fully formed in us, as once he was in Mary, we cannot grow "to mature manhood, to the measure of the stature of the fullness of Christ" (Eph. 4:13). Each exclamation consequently signifies desperate need and desperate hope. Upon his safe delivery depends our safe deliverance.

The acclamations follow the Christological titles. They share the same sublime purpose of the Magnificat: to herald the grandeur of salvation that the Son of God will bring. "You fill the universe and hold all things together"; "You appeared to Moses and gave him the law"; "You stand as an ensign for the nations"; "What you open no one can close again"; "You are the splendour of eternal light and the sun of justice"; "You are the cornerstone which makes all one"; "You are our king and judge, the Saviour."

As it considers the Nativity in the light of these messianic metaphors—drawn mostly from Isaiah (the Old Testament precursor of the first coming), and from the **Apocalypse** (which anticipates the last)—the Church sees in Mary the bearer of the Promises, and in Jesus their utter fulfillment. But in a way that surpasses expectation. His incarnation challenges our very concept of God, overturns our notion of his mighty power, topples our delusions of the Ideal

Apocalypse Another name for the Book of Revelation.

Saviour. At his long-awaited coming he revealed a Deity so small that he could not even be seen. As tiny as a fertilized ovum. So insignificant even at birth that the world disregarded him. So abject at his death that it roundly rejected him. It requires a voice of praise and proclamation—the voice of Mary long ago, the voice of the Church ever since—to lift him up high enough to be noticed and to magnify the hidden magnificence of his mercy. This is why the antiphons, like the Magnificat, are the songs of the poor in spirit. Those at the fringe of things, the unimportant, have always seen from the periphery what is missed at the core of religiously indifferent society.

It is fitting that the anthems addressed to the Virgin's Son should be sung in tune with Mary's own Canticle praising the Lord's greatness, in which she herself is declared blessed for all generations. Like garlands round an icon, the "O" antiphons adorn the Mother while adoring the Son, honour her virginal poverty along with his wealth of compassion, acknowledge jointly the simple humility of the handmaid and the humble magnanimity of her Lord.

For Reflection

1. Mary's *Magnificat* anticipates Jesus' mission. Recall some of Jesus' works and name some that can be related to Mary's description of God's work in the world.

2. Review the O Antiphons and look for parallels in their structure. Describe the three kinds of statements that make up each antiphon.

3. Of the titles given to Christ by Isaiah, echoed in the O Antiphons, which do you find most meaningful, and why?

4. We pray the O Antiphons just before Christmas. Based on your reading of Treanor, how do these prayers tie together the past, present, and future of God's people?

7 The Eternal Word Becomes Flesh

Introduction

When we think about the Christmas story, it can be so easy to get caught up in the lighthearted or charming details—the newborn lying in the manger, the farm animals gathered around him, the star shining brightly in the sky—that we can lose sight of the profound mystery the event recalls: the Second Person of the Holy Trinity, the Son of God, who took on human nature and human flesh in the womb of a human mother. This event is known as the Incarnation. We call this a mystery of faith because its inner meaning falls outside the realm of our human understanding and requires faith to be believed. Like Mary, we ask, How is this possible? More important, we ask, Why did this happen?

The two excerpts in this chapter provide some answers. Late in the second century AD, Saint Irenaeus explained the "why" of the Incarnation. Almost one thousand years later, Saint Bernard of Clairvaux preached a sermon about the same question. Such questions about the mysteries of our faith are best answered by looking at the big picture of salvation history, the story of God's life-giving actions throughout time.

All the elements of salvation history come into play in discussions about the Incarnation. God made us in his image, intending that we should live in harmony with him, with one another, and with the natural world. The sin of our first parents shattered that state of unity. Throughout history God has been promising a new life for us, in which unity and holiness will be restored. Why did the Word become flesh? To accomplish God's plan of salvation. The excerpts from Saint Irenaeus and Saint Bernard address some reasons why God's plan could only be fulfilled in this utterly surprising way.

In the first reading in this chapter, Saint Irenaeus, prompted by some **heresies** of his day, explains that sin must be eliminated from the world for God's plan of salvation to succeed. Although only God is powerful enough to overcome the stranglehold of sin, it had to be a human being who battled sin and won, as if we ourselves had to defeat sin and break its power. In Jesus Christ, the **Incarnate** Word, human and divine natures are literally united. Christ is both fully God and fully man. He alone was able to conquer sin once and for all.

But as Irenaeus points out, Christ has done so much more. In his life he was also able to reveal to us what God is really like. When we imitate Christ's actions and live according to his words, we enter into a deeper communion with the Holy Trinity. He gave his life for us and restored humanity's likeness to God, enabling us to become true images of the Divine once more. The Incarnation was the only way to restore true communion between God and humanity.

In the second selection in this chapter, from a sermon delivered in the eleventh century, Saint Bernard of Clairvaux uses the term *peace* to describe God's plan for humankind. Peace means more than the absence of strife; to live in peace means to live in harmony, to live in unity, as God originally intended. Bernard explains that throughout Old Testament history, God promised peace, often through the voices of the prophets, but people did not believe his promise. Bernard uses a metaphor, a concrete image, of abundance for God's peace; look for it in the reading. In this sermon Bernard explains that the Incarnation is the way God makes known his incredible love for humanity. By fully immersing himself in the

heresies Conscious and deliberate rejections of dogmas of the Church.

Incarnate To become flesh; specifically, God the Son assuming human nature.

incumbent Placed on someone as a duty.

human condition, by lowering himself and suffering as we do, God proves, once and for all, his astounding goodness.

In both readings in this chapter, we see that the Incarnation is the fulcrum of salvation history. Saints Irenaeus and Bernard of Clairvaux show us how the power of God's love has broken through to the history of his people in an entirely new way. From this point on, the world is changed forever, because salvation has come into the world. This is what we celebrate at Christmas: the great mystery of Emmanuel, God-with-us.

Excerpts from *Against Heresies*
By Saint Irenaeus

Book III, Chapter 18

7. Therefore, as I have already said, He [Christ] caused man (human nature) to cleave to and to become one with God. For unless man had overcome the enemy of man, the enemy would not have been legitimately vanquished. And again: unless it had been God who had freely given salvation, we could never have possessed it securely. And unless man had been joined to God, he could never have become a partaker of incorruptibility. For it was **incumbent** upon the Mediator between God and men, by His relationship to both, to bring both to friendship and concord, and present man to God, while He revealed God to man. For, in what way could we be partaken of the adoption of sons, unless we had received from

Defender of the Faith

In the second century, when the Church was still in its early days, many Christians were confused about which teachings to embrace. As bishop of Lyons, in present-day France, Saint Irenaeus was a staunch defender of the faith of the original Apostles as found in the Gospels of Matthew, Mark, Luke, and John. In his day other teachings were circulating, but Irenaeus kept calling people back to the apostolic faith of the followers of Jesus. Today scholars call Saint Irenaeus the first biblical theologian.

behoved To be required or appropriate.

Him through the Son that fellowship which refers to Himself, unless His Word, having been made flesh, had entered into communion with us? Wherefore also He passed through every stage of life, restoring to all communion with God. . . . For it **behoved** Him who was to destroy sin, and redeem man under the power of death, that He should Himself be made that very same thing which he was, that is, man; who had been drawn by sin into bondage, but was held by death, so that sin should be destroyed by man, and man should go forth from death. For as by the disobedience of the one man who was originally moulded from virgin soil, the many were made sinners (Rom. v. 19), and forfeited life; so was it necessary that, by the obedience of one man, who was originally born from a virgin, many should be justified and receive salvation. . . .

Book V, Chapter 1

1. For in no other way could we have learned the things of God, unless our Master, existing as the Word, had become man. For no other being had the power of revealing to us the things of the Father, except His own proper Word. For what other person "knew the mind of the Lord," or who else "has become His counsellor?" (Rom. xi. 34). Again, we could have learned in no other way than by seeing our Teacher, and hearing His voice with our own ears, that, having become imitators of His works as well as doers of His words, we may have communion with Him, receiving increase from the perfect One, and from Him who is prior to all creation. . . . Since the Lord thus has redeemed us through His own blood, giving His soul for our souls, and His flesh for our flesh, and has also poured out the Spirit of the Father for the union and communion of God and man, imparting indeed God to men by means of the Spirit, and, on the other hand, attaching man to God by His own incarnation, and bestowing upon us at His coming immortality durably and truly, by means of communion with God—all the doctrines of the heretics fall to ruin. . . .

Book V, Chapter 16

2. And then, again, this Word was manifested when the **Word of God** was made man, assimilating Himself to man, and man to Himself, so that by means of his resemblance to the Son, man might become precious to the Father. For in times long past, it was *said* that man was created after the image of God, but it was not [actually] *shown*; for the Word was as yet invisible, after whose image man was created, Wherefore also he did easily lose the **similitude**. When, however, the Word of God became flesh, He confirmed both these: for He both showed forth the image truly, since He became Himself what was His image; and He re-established the similitude after a sure manner, by assimilating man to the invisible Father through means of the visible Word.

> **Word of God** The entire deposit of truth God has revealed throughout history. Jesus Christ, the incarnate Son of God, is the perfect and complete Word of God (John 1:1–5).
>
> **similitude** Resemblance.

Excerpt from a Sermon, "In the Fullness of Time the Fullness of Divinity Appeared"
By Saint Bernard of Clairvaux

The goodness and humanity of God our Savior have appeared in our midst. We thank God for the many consolations he has given us during this sad exile of our pilgrimage here on earth. Before the Son of God became man his goodness was hidden, for God's mercy is eternal, but how could such goodness be recognized? It was promised, but it was not experienced, and as a result few believed in it. *Often and in many ways the Lord used to speak through the prophets.* Among other things, God said: *I think thoughts of peace and not of affliction.* But what did men respond, thinking thoughts of affliction and knowing nothing of peace? They said: *Peace, peace, there is no peace.* This response made the *angels of peace weep bitterly,* saying: *Lord, who has believed our message?* But now men believe because they see with their own eyes, and because God's *testimony has now become even more credible.* He has gone so far as to *pitch his tent in the sun* so even the dimmest eyes see him.

Notice that peace is not promised but sent to us; it is no longer deferred, it is given; peace is not prophesied but achieved. It is as if God the Father sent upon the earth a purse full of his mercy. This purse was burst open during the Lord's passion to pour forth its hidden contents—the price of our redemption. It was only a small purse, but it was very full. As the Scriptures tell us: *A little child has been given to us, but in him dwells all the fullness of the divine nature.* The fullness of time brought with it the fullness of divinity. God's Son came in the flesh so that mortal men could see and recognize God's kindness. When God reveals his humanity, his goodness cannot possibly remain hidden. To show his kindness what more could he do beyond taking my human form? My humanity, I say, not Adam's—that is, not such as he had before his fall.

How could he have shown his mercy more clearly than by taking on himself our condition? For our sake the Word of God became as grass. What better proof could he have given of his love? Scripture says: *Lord, what is man that you are mindful of him; why does your heart go out to him?* The incarnation teaches us how much God cares for us and what he thinks and feels about us. We should stop thinking of our own sufferings and remember what he has suffered. Let us think of all the Lord has done for us, and then we shall realize how his goodness

> 66 *The incarnation teaches us how much God cares for us and what he thinks and feels about us.* 99

appears through his humanity. The lesser he became through his human nature the greater was his goodness; the more he lowered himself for me, the dearer he is to me. *The goodness and humanity of God our Savior have appeared,* says the Apostle.

Truly great and manifest are the goodness and humanity of God. He has given us a most wonderful proof of his goodness by adding humanity to his own divine nature.

For Reflection

1. What are some results, or effects, of the Incarnation that Irenaeus notes?

2. Recall the "big picture" of salvation history, beginning with God's creation of humanity in his own image. How is Church teaching about humanity's creation and the Fall reflected in Irenaeus's teaching on the Incarnation?

3. What metaphor does Bernard use to describe the abundance of God's peace? How does the image relate to prophecies about the coming Messiah? How does it help us understand our redemption through the cross?

8 The Son Reveals the Father

Introduction

When Jesus Christ, the Word of God, "became flesh / and made his dwelling among us" (John 1:14), he allowed us to discover God in a new, previously unfathomable way. God has been revealing himself throughout history, but it is beyond our human abilities to grasp who he is and his immense goodness and glory. God is truly beyond our human understanding. So how can we come to know God? We can learn through his Son, the Word Incarnate: Jesus Christ. Jesus can do more than tell us about God; he alone can show us God.

In this chapter Fr. Marie-Dominique Philippe, a twentieth-century Dominican philosopher and theologian, explains how Jesus shows us the Father. He starts by pointing out that others acted as the Father's emissaries before the birth of Jesus, delivering the Father's message; we read the words of these prophets in the Old Testament. But Jesus is unique because he is more than an **emissary**—he is also the Beloved Son of the Father.

> ### Philosopher, Theologian, and Founder
>
> In the 1970s Fr. Marie-Dominique Philippe founded three religious communities, collectively known as the Family of Saint John. More than one thousand religious brothers and sisters in five countries belong to the order, along with 2,500 secular oblates, who are married or single people living outside the community. Philippe himself remained a Dominican until his death in 2006.

emissary Representative or agent.

Philippe explains that Jesus' mission went beyond that of any of the prophets. Rather, he says, Christ came to reveal "the secrets He had received from the Father that the Father wants to show us."

Secrets? Have we been missing some hidden message when we read the Gospels? No, Philippe means that what Jesus reveals can only be revealed by him, because Jesus himself is the message as well as the messenger. Jesus does more than simply tell us about God's love. Jesus fully reveals and embodies God's love. He himself *is* God; he himself *is* Love. And he wants to bring us closer to the Father, the source of love.

This excerpt from an interview with Philippe includes the Greek word *agapetos* (ah-gah-pay-*toss*) in reference to Jesus. *Agapetos*, meaning "beloved one," appears in the Gospel narratives about Jesus' Baptism and Transfiguration. The Epistles of John also use the word *agapetos* to address the reader: "Beloved, let us love one another" (1 John 4:7). In biblical Greek the root word *agape* refers to love—but *agape* is different from the love found in ordinary friendship, and it is also not the same as romantic attraction (called *eros*). Scholars sometimes describe *agape* as self-giving, unconditional love that wants what is truly best for another. *Agape* is the truest and deepest love: the kind of love that God has for us.

The Gospel of John relates that after Jesus died, but before his body was removed from the cross, a soldier pierced his side with a lance (see John 19:33–34). In this reading Philippe suggests that the wound to Jesus' heart represents a particular

> ### Jesus, the Son
>
> The term *beloved Son* appears in Gospel accounts of two events: Jesus' Baptism and Transfiguration. When Jesus is baptized, the heavens open, the Holy Spirit descends on him, and a voice proclaims him God's beloved Son (Mark 1:10–11). The same pronouncement is also heard when Jesus is transfigured before three disciples, who see him flanked by the great prophets Moses and Elijah, his face and garments radiant with light. Again the voice identifies Jesus as his beloved Son (Matthew 17:1–5, Mark 9:2–7, Luke 9:28–35).

demonstration of his love for us. The devotion to the Sacred Heart of Jesus derives from this detail of the Crucifixion because the pierced heart represents Jesus' *agape*—his total gift of self—for humanity.

Philippe also examines the idea of the face of Jesus, bringing into focus the mystery of the union of Jesus' divine and human natures: the mystery of the Incarnation. Jesus is fully divine and fully human, and these two natures are never separated. Jesus told his disciples, "Whoever has seen me has seen the Father" (John 14:9). Yet Jesus' face is also that of a man. Philippe concludes that God wished for "the face of man [to] become his face." Though Jesus certainly reveals the Father to us, he also reveals the true nature of humanity to us—that is, humanity united to God.

Excerpt from an Interview (conducted in March 1989 by the Catholic Communications Network, in Corpus Christi, Texas)

By Fr. Marie-Dominique Philippe, OP

"For God so loved the world that he sent his only Son" (Jn 3:16). Jesus is the one sent by the Father to us. The prophets have all come as men sent by God; they possessed in themselves something which was beyond them. All the great prophets of the First Covenant—Isaiah, Ezekiel, Amos, all of them—are witnesses, envoys. And it is written that, for us, Jesus is truly the emissary of the Father. St. John continuously shows us that Jesus is the one sent and the faithful witness. But Jesus is also the Beloved Son. Only the Beloved Son can fully reveal to us who the Father is. An envoy reveals what a lord, a master, is, what someone who has authority is; but a son, especially if he is the Beloved Son, or even a friend, reveals to us his secrets. The Son is sent not only to fulfill a task. He has indeed come for that purpose, yet He has come for something still greater. He has come to reveal to us the secrets that He has received from the Father and that the Father wants to show us. This is why He does not hesitate to say to His apostles: "You are no longer my servants but my friends." Each Christian, in his Christian life, becomes aware of this double relationship: he is at the same time an envoy, a servant, who ought to accomplish a task, but he also understands at a given moment that this is not enough, that there is something even greater: this bond of love, in his most intimate heart, with Jesus and with the Father. It is perhaps there that we touch the great secret of our Christian life: Jesus is a witness of the truth. He said so, and He said so before Pilate, therefore before someone who didn't have Christian faith, someone who exercised authority and who had a sense of this truth, a truth which is completely unique: He is the Truth. He is the Truth because He is the Beloved Son of the Father who is love. He reveals to us the absolute goal of our Christian life, which is the love of the Father for His Son and the love of the Son for His Father. This covenant goes beyond all others, and it is a very simple covenant because it is a covenant of love. But it is also the most demanding covenant. The demands of the Law only prepare us for these greater demands of love. And truly, for us as believers, as Christians, Jesus is the Beloved Son of the Father.

There is a very powerful Greek name, which I am very fond of: the "agapetos." Jesus is the friend par excellence; He is the one who has been loved the most and who is always the most loved, because this love is a divine love which is always real. Jesus is the one most loved by the Father. The entire **physiognomy** of Jesus, His entire earthly life in the midst of us, whether it be His hidden life, His public life or, and especially, the mystery of the Cross and Resurrection, shows us the mystery of the aga-petos, of the Beloved Son. Jesus is not the beloved of men but the Beloved of the Father. He is the Beloved One, and this name sums up everything; we need to begin from it and come back to it always. The whole of Jesus' life shows us the particular modalities, special words or particular gestures through which this name is revealed to us: Jesus is the Beloved One. It is perhaps for this reason that Saint John wanted to show that the last and ultimate moment of Revelation is the wound of Jesus' heart, which is a gesture. . . . It is a gesture which wounds Jesus' heart in order to unveil to us the unique depth of love which is hidden in the heart of Christ and which exer-cises a very strong attraction

physiognomy External appearance that provides an indication of character.

upon us: Jesus is not only a perfect being, a being who is irreproachable in Himself; Jesus is not only an innocent being; He is the Beloved one—He is Love. And it is for this reason that He attracts us. He states it Himself: "And I, when I am lifted up from the earth, will draw all men to myself" (Jn 12:32). It is perhaps there that we grasp better this powerful, unique attraction that Jesus holds over us.

But we have to allow it to happen to us, and we have to have a strong desire to discover what is most profound in Him. I would like to reflect quickly on this, since it concerns in fact the whole Gospel and particularly the Gospel of St. John. From the very beginning, St. John tells us that the Son remains in the Father's heart. It is quite daring and marvelous to state that the Son remains in the source, the heart of the Father, the source of all fruitfulness, the source of all love, the secret source. The Son remains in the heart of the Father, and the Son who remains in the heart of the Father is the fruit of the Father's contemplation, of His Wisdom. He is the Word, and He is also the one who is given to us. He is the one who gives us the whole mystery of the Father's fruitfulness, the whole mystery of His love.

If we reflect for a moment on the Baptism of Jesus and His Transfiguration, we are awed by this presence of the Father; but we are even more awed by the presence of the Father at the Cross: there is a silence from the Father. And this indeed raises a big question for us about which we will try to speak. At Jesus' Baptism, the Father says, "This is my beloved Son, with whom I am well pleased" (Matt 3:17). At the Transfiguration, the Father says the same thing, but He also wants us to understand that we ought to listen to Jesus, to understand Him, to be eager to receive everything He says, since He is the one who teaches us about love. Jesus is the master of love, and it is He who, through His whole teaching and all His gestures, never ceases to lead us towards being beloved children of the Father. He has chosen us, and He has loved us first; and we need to respond to His love. He has brought us near to the Father, the source of all true love. . . .

Disappointments in the order of love are what are most terrible; they destroy the heart. Someone who has given himself fully in love, and who has been left disappointed, is deeply wounded. Jesus was deeply given over to each one of His apostles, to each one, even to Judas, and He accepted their betrayal, through love of us, in order to show us that His love is victorious even over betrayal, and that to give oneself over to Him is to give oneself over to the Father. This is precisely what He said in a very powerful way to the Apostle Philip who asked him the question, "Show us the Father." Jesus answered, "Philip, he who sees me, sees the Father" (Jn 14:9). This expression has an astonishing force, as if the face of the Father for us was the face of Jesus. The face of Jesus is a man's face. He is the Son of man, and He is the son of Mary—He resembles His mother, as we all resemble our mothers. But He resembles His mother in a unique way since He had only one human heredity and since Mary was immaculate. There was therefore a unique resemblance between Jesus and His Mother. It is extraordinary to realize that the face of Jesus is the face of Mary, of the woman, of the woman *par excellence* and that His face is also the face of the Father for us. The gaze of Jesus is the gaze of the Father. Looking at Jesus, being attentive to Him, in His crib, this poor child's crib in Bethlehem, looking at Him next to Joseph working in his workshop, looking at Him adoring in the desert, looking at Him preaching and teaching, looking at Him

> *It is always the face of the Father present in the face of Jesus, and this face is also the face of man: it is our face.*

especially when He is completely disfigured on the Cross, when He no longer has a man's face—it is always the face of the Father present in the face of Jesus, and this face is also the face of man: it is our face. God willed to do that. God, who is our Creator, who has formed us, and who wanted us to be His masterpiece, willed that the face of man should become His face. I believe that this is what Jesus wanted to teach us through this great revelation in the Gospel: He is the Beloved Son of the Father, for us.

For Reflection

1. Based on this reading, how is Jesus like the prophets of the Old Testament? What sets him apart from the prophets?

2. What tasks does the ordinary Christian share with Jesus, according to Philippe?

3. What does Philippe mean when he says that God wishes that "the face of man" should become God's face?

Part 3
Christ, the Light of the World

9 Jesus Resists Temptation

Introduction

We all can relate to the story of Jesus' temptation in the desert. Each of us has had to take a stand against allurements that contradict our own sense of God's will for us. The temptation narrative in the Gospel of Matthew, the first excerpt in this chapter, relates Jesus' experience in the desert, where he had to remain true to his mission and to God's will for him in the face of the devil's temptation. God had called Jesus to prepare for his mission in solitude. Matthew tells us that Jesus spent forty days praying and fasting in the desert. During this time the devil tempted Jesus three times. *Turn these stones into bread, you must be hungry! Leap off the Temple wall and allow God's angels to catch you! Bow down and worship me!* Each time, Jesus countered the temptation with words from Scripture. Finally Satan departed.

Fr. Daniel Harrington, a Scripture scholar and New Testament professor at Boston College, offers an explanation of this passage from Matthew in the second excerpt here, taken from his biblical commentary titled *The Gospel of Matthew*. Because we all understand the human experience of being tempted, one way we could approach the Scripture passage recounting Jesus' temptation is to reflect on what Jesus may have been thinking when he was tempted. But Harrington comes at the story from a different angle. He writes about the Gospel writer's intention in relating this story. Harrington explains that the narrative helps to establish the identity of Jesus as the Son of God early in the Gospel.

The first-century audience Matthew was addressing—mostly Jews who had come to believe in Jesus—would have been familiar with the Hebrew Scriptures that we call the Old Testament. Matthew's audience would have not only recognized the passages Jesus quotes in the temptation narrative but also understood the context and message of those passages and recognized echoes of their own history.

For these early Jewish Christians, the story of Jesus' temptation in the desert probably related to more than just the universal human experience of being tempted. In particular, they likely recalled that the Hebrew people, in their earliest days as a covenant community, had their own experience of being led through the desert for forty years before entering the Promised Land. Harrington explains that because Jesus replies to the devil by quoting verses from the Book of Deuteronomy, Matthew's Jewish readers would have recalled that book's explanation for the time of wandering: namely, that God was testing them to see if they would be faithful to his Commandments. Indeed much of the Old Testament shows that God's People were not always faithful to him after their arrival in the Promised Land; they continually turned to idol worship and ignored God's Law. According to Harrington, the temptation narrative in the Gospel of Matthew allowed these Jewish followers of Jesus to see that God's Chosen Son responded to the Father's call to mission in a way that God's Chosen People had failed to do.

Harrington's analysis places the story of Jesus' temptation firmly in the larger context of salvation history, showing that Jesus is the culmination of God's saving work that began with his Chosen People in the Old Testament. The selection illustrates the

> ### What's Up with Forty?
>
> In the Bible, numbers tie together narratives from different periods in salvation history, and they have symbolic meanings too. Both the Israelites' desert wanderings and Jesus' time in the desert involve preparation for a new beginning, a biblical theme associated with the number forty. Other examples include the forty years Moses stayed away from Egypt after killing an overseer, as well as the forty days in which Jesus continued to appear after the Resurrection. What new beginnings followed these events?

importance of reading the Gospels against the backdrop of the Old Testament—and of understanding the historical context, purpose, and audience of each Gospel and its writer.

Matthew 4:1–11

Then Jesus was led by the Spirit into the desert to be tempted by the devil. He fasted for forty days and forty nights, and afterwards he was hungry. The tempter approached and said to him, "If you are the Son of God, command that these stones become loaves of bread."

He said in reply, "It is written:

'One does not live by bread alone,
    but by every word that comes forth from the
        mouth of God.'"

Then the devil took him to the holy city, and made him stand on the parapet of the temple, and said to him, "If you are the Son of God, throw yourself down. For it is written:

'He will command his angels concerning you'
    and 'with their hands they will support you,
lest you dash your foot against a stone.'"

Jesus answered him, "Again it is written, 'You shall not put the Lord, your God, to the test.'" Then the devil took him up to a very high mountain, and showed him all the kingdoms of the world in their magnificence, and he said to him, "All these I shall give to you, if you will prostrate yourself and worship me." At this, Jesus said to him, "Get away, Satan! It is written:

'The Lord, your God, shall you worship
    and him alone shall you serve.'"

Then the devil left him and, behold, angels came and ministered to him.

Excerpt from *The Gospel of Matthew*

By Daniel J. Harrington, SJ

Interpretation

The customary title for Matt 4:1–11 and its parallels (Mark 1:12–13; Luke 4:1–13) is the "Temptation of Jesus." A better title, one more appropriate to the biblical basis of the narrative in the Book of Deuteronomy, is the "Testing of God's Son." The concern of the passage

> ❝ *Where Israel in the wilderness failed, Jesus passes every test.* ❞

is not so much whether the devil can lure Jesus into this or that sin as it is the portrayal of Jesus as God's Son "who in every respect has been tested as we are, yet without sin" (Heb 4:15). Where Israel in the wilderness failed, Jesus passes every test. . . .

After a narrative introduction (Matt 4:1–2), the Matthean version [of the story] consists of three dialogues between the devil and Jesus (4:3–4, 5–7, 8–10) and a narrative conclusion (4:11). Each dialogue has the devil offering a test and Jesus responding with a quotation from Deuteronomy 6–8. . . .

The three biblical quotations in which Jesus' responses are expressed come from Deuteronomy 6–8 (8:3; 6:16; 6:13). In those chapters Moses addresses the people of Israel near the end of their wandering in the wilderness and before their entrance into the promised land. The underlying motif of the Book of Deuteronomy is the covenant. In chapters 6–8 Moses supplies the historical foundations for God's relationship with Israel and presents **exhortations** on that basis. . . .

The premise of Moses' speech is God's love for and election of Israel: "The Lord your God has chosen you to be a people for his own possession . . . because the Lord loves you" (Deut 7:6–7). The relationship between God and Israel takes the form of a covenant: "the faithful God who keeps covenant and steadfast love with

exhortations Words that move listeners to action.

those who love him and keep his commandments" (Deut 7:9). Woven through the speech are references to Israel's wanderings in the wilderness and the challenges related to its entrance into the promised land. These are placed in the context of a father-son relationship: "As a man disciplines his son, the Lord your God disciplines you" (Deut 8:5). The motif of Israel as God's son appears elsewhere in this book (see Deut 1:31; 14:1; 32:5–6, 18–20) and other OT [Old Testament] writings (see Exod 4:22–23; Hos 11:1).

Israel's experience in the wilderness is expressed in terms of a test from God: "And you shall remember all the way which the Lord your God has led you these forty years in the wilderness, that he might humble you, testing you to know what was in your heart, whether you would keep his commandments, or not" (Deut 8:2). Besides the testing motif this verse contains several other themes developed in Matt 4:1–11: Israel's being led by God, the number forty, the wilderness, and perhaps even the notion of fasting in the verb "humble" ('nh).

Whereas God may test Israel, Israel should not test God: "You shall not put the Lord your God to the test, as you tested him at Massah" (Deut 6:16). By quoting this verse in Matt 4:7 Jesus aligns himself with Israel as it should be and in contrast to Israel as it was at **Massah and Meribah** (see Exod 17:1–7).

So Deuteronomy 6–8 not only supplies the three biblical quotations attributed to Jesus in Matt 4:1–11 but also provides the key terms "Son of God" (see Matt 4:3, 6) and "test." Moses challenges Israel to learn from its past mistakes in the wilderness and to act faithfully as it enters the Promised Land. Matthew . . . presents Jesus as the true Son of God who passes the tests set forth by the devil and emerges as the model of covenant fidelity.

Massah and Meribah Names meaning "testing place" and "quarreling place," respectively; where Moses accused the people of testing God in Exodus 17:1–7.

rabbinic Relating to rabbis or their teachings.

. . . [Matthew's] version of the "Testing of God's Son" . . . was an especially congenial text for him and his audience. In form it resembles a **rabbinic** debate in which great teachers trade quotations from Scripture and settle arguments by them. In content it carries on Matthew's attempt to identify Jesus before the beginning of his public ministry. The idea of Jesus as God's Son had already been raised in Matt 1:20; 2:15; and 3:17. The testing narrative allows Matthew to connect Jesus' divine sonship with the experience of Israel. Israel in the wilderness failed the testing; Jesus passes it.

The contrast between the wilderness generation and Jesus need not lead to talk about Jesus as the "new Israel." Rather Jesus stands with Israel in accepting the challenges posed by Moses in Deuteronomy 6–8. . . . Far from replacing Israel, Jesus takes his identity from Israel. Behind the early Christian claims about his divine sonship is his solidarity with the Israel addressed by Moses. He accepts the testing from God and refuses to test God. . . .

In the Church's calendar, Matt 4:1–11 becomes prominent at the beginning of Lent. Understanding this text against the background of Deuteronomy 6–8 allows one to go beyond the narrow themes of fasting and temptation to the level of **Christology**. As is the case with all the material in the opening chapters of Matthew, the focus of attention is the identity of Jesus. Understanding it as the testing of God's Son allows one to see the nature of Jesus' divine sonship and its relation to Israel as God's Son.

> **Christology** The systematic statement of Christian beliefs about Jesus Christ, including his identity, mission, and saving work on earth.

For Reflection

1. In the reading from Matthew, Jesus responds to the devil in the desert three times. What three points about faithfulness to God does Jesus make?

2. Harrington turns to the Old Testament Book of Deuteronomy to consider why the Israelites wandered in the desert for forty years. Based on Harrington's discussion, explain in your own words why the Israelites were forced to wander in the wilderness for so long.

3. Although he contrasts the experiences of the Israelites and Jesus in their desert wanderings, Harrington argues against the idea that Jesus replaces Israel. How does Harrington see Jesus' relationship to Israel?

10 Parables of the Kingdom

Introduction

Do you recall the Parable of the Lost Sheep? It is one of Jesus' most familiar teachings:

> What man among you having a hundred sheep and losing one of them would not leave the ninety-nine in the desert and go after the lost one until he finds it? And when he does find it, he sets it on his shoulders with great joy and, upon his arrival home, he calls together his friends and neighbors and says to them, "Rejoice with me because I have found my lost sheep." I tell you, in just the same way there will be more joy in heaven over one sinner who repents than over ninety-nine righteous people who have no need of repentance. (Luke 15:4–7)

Now picture the audience's response. Those who raise sheep sagely nod their heads. "Of course we would search for a sheep that became separated from the flock," they say to one another. "Yes, we would be very happy to find it. That's just common sense." Then comes the kicker. In the same way, Jesus says, God rejoices over each sinner who repents. Confusion crosses the faces of the crowd. They begin to murmur: "Wait—God cares about sinners? He actually goes looking for them and rejoices when he finds them?" Then you may even note annoyance on some faces, as people express amazement: "He cares as much about a sinner as he does about *me*?" And finally, perhaps, a look of wonder: "Incredible!"

Megan McKenna is a storyteller as well as a theologian. In her book *Parables: Arrows of God,* she tells her own **parables** to explain Jesus' storytelling technique. Jesus' parables—the Lost Sheep, the Prodigal Son, the Good Samaritan, and others—are so familiar that we may miss the element of surprise, even shock, that characterizes parables. Jesus used these simple tales, based on everyday life, to challenge his listeners. The stories had the power to jolt first-century audiences into a new way of thinking, as McKenna's stories do for us in the excerpt here.

Because McKenna's tales are new, the endings are able to surprise us, to pull us up short. We can also understand the context of McKenna's modern parables, just as those listening to Jesus understood a context related to herding sheep, scattering seed, baking bread, and working in a vineyard. Reading McKenna's parables gives us a taste of what Jesus' listeners experienced.

Well-constructed parables do surprise us, but they also challenge us. It is not possible to really hear a parable without also hearing a call to action. Implicit in each parable is the question, What will *you* do? Do you see this challenge in the Parable of the Lost Sheep? Grasping this challenge would be the final response of those listening to Jesus: "If this is how God responds to sinners, how will I respond to them?"

McKenna's modern parables illustrate how Jesus' storytelling worked, but they also reflect the underlying theme of Jesus' parables, the **Kingdom of God**, also called the Kingdom of Heaven. Although the fullness of God's Kingdom will not be realized until the end of time, Jesus announces the Kingdom and also embodies it. That is because the Kingdom is the reign or rule of God over our hearts; Jesus lived that reality every day. When God reigns over the hearts of all, we will enjoy a world ruled by unconditional love.

parables Stories rooted in daily life that use symbolism or allegory as a teaching tool and that usually have a surprise ending.

Kingdom of God The rule of God over the hearts of people and, as a consequence of that, the development of a new social order based on unconditional love.

McKenna's parables communicate that we are called to cooperate with God to bring about his Kingdom. Her parables help us to see the truth—about ourselves and about others. The stories challenge us to think about the part we will play in God's plan to bring about a world where unconditional love reigns. McKenna calls Jesus' parables "arrows of God" because, she says, they point to the Kingdom.

Excerpt from *Parables: The Arrows of God*

By Megan McKenna

- Once upon a time there was an old man who lived on the outskirts of a town. He had lived there so long that no one knew who he was or where he had come from. Some said that once he had been very powerful, a king, but that was long ago. Others said, no, he was once very wealthy and generous, but without much now. Others said, no, he was wise and influential, and some even said he was holy. But the children just thought he was a stupid old man, and they made his life miserable. They threw stones at his windows, left dead cats on his doorstep, ripped up his garden, and shouted at him every chance they got.

  Then one day an older boy came up with an idea to prove once and for all that their parents were wrong, that he wasn't wealthy, or once a king, or wise or holy, that he was just a stupid old man. He knew how to catch a bird in a snare. He told the other children that he would catch a bird, and together they'd go to the old man's house and knock on his door. When the man answered, he would ask him, "Old man, do you know what I have hidden behind my back?" Now, he might guess that it's a bird, but it's the second question that will get him. I'll ask him if the bird is dead or alive. If he says dead, then I'll just let the bird go free. If he answers that the bird is alive, then I'll just crush the bird to death in my hands. Either way, he's just a stupid old man.

The kids thought it was a great idea. The older boy caught the bird and off they went to the old man's house and rudely knocked on the door. The old man came to the door, looked around at all the children and knew they were up to something. The boy spoke quickly, "Old man, do you know what I have hidden behind my back?" The old man looked around at the children one by one and out of the corner of his eye he saw a white feather fall to the ground. He answered, "Yes, I do. It's a bird, a white bird." The children's eyes grew large. He could have guessed it was a bird, but how did he know it was white? Maybe their parents were right about him after all. But the leader was not to be deterred and quickly asked the second question. "Well, that was a good guess, but is the bird dead or alive?" Again, the old man looked around at each child, sadly, and finally his eyes came to rest on the older boy. He answered, "That all depends on you. The answer is in your hands."

A parable, contemporary or traditional or scriptural, causes stark and unexpected reactions. A parable causes an emotional response, evoking fear, loneliness, sorrow, horror, because the parable always throws the ending, the reality, the circumstances back into our lap. We react almost viscerally—"No, tell me what to do. No, it can't be. No, you don't mean. . . . Do I have to decide right now? Can we discuss this?" Whenever the truth hits us hard, it hits us in our stomach. That's why parables are often difficult to put on a page after you've heard the story, swallowed it and nearly choked on it.

> *If we don't make the good news come true in the world, then it dies.*

Parables always go for the truth at the heart of the matter. In fact, every time we read the scriptures liturgically we can end by saying, "It all depends. The answer is in our hands." Whether or not the scriptures come true is up to us. Jesus came, proclaimed the good news, lived the good news, is the good news, and now he has entrusted the good news to us. If we don't make the good news come true in the world, then it dies. God trusts us a lot more than we would choose!

Sometimes we hear all the small details in a parable and fail to go for the heart of the matter. . . . We side-step the important point and hear the story from our limited and rather biased perceptions.

Often parables make us angry. There may be anger about others' behavior and attitudes. But, at root, we are angry at ourselves. The parable tells us the truth in some way about ourselves. Parables and the whole of scripture are truth-tellers. The text exposes us before ourselves and others.

Most of us want to be dealt with individually, not in a group, or classified as belonging to the human race or the various groups we are affiliated with. But parables and the gospels always say that we are all sinners, we are all in the same boat, and we have to look at this together because we either go down together or rise together. The parables of Jesus make us angry, sad, glad, nervous, because they tell us the truth about what we claim to be, even though the truth may not be apparent from our behavior, attitudes and alliances.

The parables do many things to us. But ultimately we want the stories to be good news. We want goodness, justice and right to triumph. In the tale above, we want the old man to triumph, even though he has to put up with a lot before he finally does. The role we take on in the story is always pivotal: the old man, the youth, the other children, the neighborhood, even the bird. The old man, the underdog, a respect for age, a sense of camaraderie because of exclusion, solitariness. We go for the one we are attracted to, that we think is like us, the one misjudged. We listen in the story for a glimpse of recognition.

> **A Master Storyteller**
>
> Jesus did not invent the teaching method of the parable. Many wise teachers throughout the Mediterranean world taught in parables. The Greek philosophers Plato and Aristotle both used parables; so did Jewish rabbis in biblical commentary. The Old Testament contains a handful of parables, including one that the prophet Nathan told to make King David realize the seriousness of the king's sin with Bathsheba (2 Samuel 12:1–4). Scholars tell us that Jesus was a master of the form, perhaps giving us the most compelling parables ever told.

Listeners can also be the bird, the nonhuman one, the helpless one, the victim, the one used by the others. Then there is the older boy, the one who is the center, pulling the attention, looking for status, power, proving his point. We can often hear this story, and others, from this point of view, but we don't admit to it readily. And there are the other children, just waiting to see what will happen, playing it safe, secure. The parables work like this.

- There was a woman who wanted peace in the world and peace in her heart and all sorts of good things, but she was very frustrated. The world seemed to be falling apart. She would read the papers and get depressed. One day she decided to go shopping, and she went into a mall and picked a store at random. She walked in and was surprised to see Jesus behind the counter. She knew it was Jesus, because he looked just like the pictures she'd seen on holy cards and devotional pictures. She looked again and again at him, and finally she got up her nerve and asked, "Excuse me, are you Jesus?" "I am." "Do you work here?" "No," Jesus said, "I own the store." "Oh, what do you sell in here?" "Oh, just about anything!" "Anything?" "Yeah, anything you want. What do you want?" She said, "I don't know." "Well," Jesus said, "feel free, walk up and down the aisles, make a list, see what it is you want, and then come back and we'll see what we can do for you."

  She did just that, walked up and down the aisles. There was peace on earth, no more war, no hunger or poverty, peace in families, no more drugs, harmony, clean air, careful use of resources. She wrote furiously. By the time she got back to the counter, she had a long list. Jesus took the list, skimmed through it, looked up at her and smiled. "No problem." And then he bent down behind the counter and picked out all sorts of things, stood up, and laid out the packets. She asked, "What are these?" Jesus replied, "Seed packets. This is a catalog store." She said, "You mean I don't get the finished product?" "No, this is a place of dreams. You come and see what it looks like, and I give you the seeds. You plant the seeds. You go home and nurture them and help them to grow and someone else reaps the benefits." "Oh," she said. And she left the store without buying anything.

If we don't get what we want right away, then maybe we don't really want it, or we don't want it enough. This is discouraging. We may have seen the dream of the kingdom. We may know exactly how the kingdom comes, but that doesn't mean that we bring it, or contribute to it, or are a part of it. We are all reaping the benefits of those who have gone before us in faith and life. But we need to stop and ask ourselves what we are doing for others. What seeds are we planting and nourishing? Our religion teaches that it is not primarily what we do for ourselves or our own, but what we do for others, for the outsiders, the strangers, that reveals our belief.

For Reflection

1. The characters in McKenna's parables display traits we might find distasteful. What darker aspects of the human character—of ourselves—do these parables force us to confront?

2. McKenna says that parables hit us on a gut level. What emotions does she intend for us to experience while reading the parable about the children's visit to the old man?

3. How would you like McKenna's parable of the children and the old man to end? Why? What would your desired ending illustrate about the Kingdom of God?

4. McKenna says that parables challenge us, throwing the ending "back into our lap." What does the parable about the woman in the store challenge us to do? What specific action could you, a high school student, take in response?

11 The Miracles as Signs

Introduction

In a poll conducted for *Newsweek* in 2000, 84 percent of those surveyed said they believe God performs miracles, and almost half of those surveyed said they had witnessed a miracle (*Los Angeles Times*, May 6, 2000). Those eyewitnesses to miracles must have responded with amazement and gratitude. But would it not be interesting to know what they thought about the meaning of the miracle they witnessed? We could ask them, "What did that miracle tell you about God?" Some might answer that God is moved to compassion by our prayers. Some might say that God sends us signs so we can grow in faith. Others might answer that he wants to assure us that the powers of darkness will not win in the end. Could all of these answers be correct?

In *The Miracles of Jesus and the Theology of Miracles*, theologian and Jesuit priest René Latourelle looks closely at how miracles reported in the Gospels function as signs that point to greater truths about God. We are not used to thinking of someone's actions—in this case, miracles performed by Jesus—as

> **The Work of the Theologian**
>
> A theologian is someone who engages in systematic study of Divine Revelation about God. To use a phrase coined in the Middle Ages, theologians do all of their work "standing on the shoulders of giants"; that is, before formulating their own ways to explain the truths revealed in Sacred Scripture and Church Tradition, they carefully study the work of those who went before. Their work becomes part of the Church's shared wisdom, rooted in centuries of scholarship.

signs pointing to a greater truth. But remember that Jesus reveals the Father to us. He shows us God.

Latourelle discusses many theological truths conveyed by Jesus' miracles, emphasizing that the miracles point to several different truths at once. In the excerpt you will read here, Latourelle examines three of the many "sign values" or theological truths about God and explains how the Gospel miracles reveal these truths. First, he says, miracles show us that God has real power. Second, they show that God is always loving. And third, they show that the Kingdom of God is present in Jesus, the Messiah.

Latourelle's close analysis of the viewpoints seen in different Gospels reminds us that the Gospels were never intended to be historical accounts or play-by-play reports. Biblical scholars understand that the Gospels developed over time within the believing community. They do relate the events of Jesus' life, but they also offer a theological interpretation of the meaning of those events.

Looking for the sign values, or truths, that the miracles reveal can help us stay focused on the right question about Jesus. Instead of asking, How is that possible? we can ask, What does this mean? Uncovering the truths the miracles point to—and there may be more than one—can deepen our faith by increasing our understanding of God's unfolding plan of salvation.

Excerpt from *The Miracles of Jesus and the Theology of Miracles*

By René Latourelle

Miracles are . . . polyvalent signs; that is, they act on several levels at once, and they point in several directions. The New Testament is the best witness to this plurality and diversity of sign values which miracles display. . . .

I. Sign Values

1. Signs of the Power of God

This meaning is already present in the words used in describing miracles. These are works proper to God and impossible to human beings *(adynata),* manifestations and effects of the divine power *(dynameis),* works *(erga)* of God and of Christ as Son of the Father.[1] Looked at in their source and therefore as works and acts of power, miracles are part of the great work which God began at creation and brought to completion in redemption. . . . Miracles are **epiphanies** of God the Savior, expressions of the **efficacy** of his saving word.

This central theme is the same in all four **evangelists** but it is handled by each with nuances peculiar to him. In *Mark* miracles issue from the person of Jesus and from the power that acts in him: a power capable of transforming the entire human person, body and soul, and of dismantling the kingdom of Satan in order to establish the reign of God. But the exercise of this power is limited by the self-abasement of the Son of Man. The helplessness of Jesus in the face of human

epiphanies Visible demonstrations of God's presence in the world.

efficacy Efficiency; ability to produce a desired result.

evangelists Based on a word for "good news"; here, the persons traditionally recognized as authors of the four Gospels: Matthew, Mark, Luke, and John.

rejection and hatred and his weakness during the passion reveal the depths of his humble, humiliated love. The true limitation of his power is due to his love, which causes him to surrender himself for the salvation of all (Mk 6:1–6).

In the eyes of *Matthew* Jesus is the Lord whose intervention is sovereign, instantaneous, and universal. Christ (Mt 8–9) has authority over sickness, death, the wind, the sea, and Satan. His dominion over evil is unqualified. He has delegated this power to the apostles and the Church, because "all authority" in heaven and on earth has been given to him (Mt 28:18).

According to *Luke* miracles are "visitations" of God who thereby makes himself known and saves (Lk 7:16). They proclaim complete and definitive salvation. In *John,* finally, miracles are joint works of the Father and the Son; they show that power resides in Christ as it does in the Father. Christ is God himself present among us, exercising, like the Father, the power that raises up and gives life (Jn 5:21). Christ's glory is the glory of Yahweh himself.[2]

2. Signs of the Agape of God

Miracles are not mere displays of power, for this power is itself in the service of love. Christ's miracles are manifestations of his active, compassionate love that stoops to alleviate every form of affliction. In him "the goodness and loving kindness of God our Savior appeared" (Tit 3:4).

Sometimes the initiative comes directly from Christ who anticipates the pleas of human beings, as in the multiplication of the loaves (Mk 6:34), the raising of the widow's son at Nain (Lk 7:13), and the healings of the man with a withered hand (Lk 6:6–7), the crippled woman (Lk 13:11–12), and the invalid at the Pool of Bethzatha (Jn 5:5–9). Other miracles, however, are responses of Christ to petitions that are sometimes expressed in so many words, sometimes tacitly implied in a gesture or action. The blind men at Jericho ask that their eyes be opened (Mt 20:29–34); the Canaanite woman wins the desired healing by her persistence (Mt 15:21–28); the leper falls on his knees and implores Jesus (Mk 1:40–41); the centurion (Lk 7:3), Jairus (Lk 8:40–42), the father of the epileptic boy

(Lk 9:38–42), and Martha and Mary (Jn 11:3) all beg Jesus to intervene in their favor. But the woman with a hemorrhage (Mk 5:27) and the people of the area around Gennesaret (Mt 14:36) only touch the hem of Jesus' garment and are healed.

All these healings and raisings from the dead are actions inspired by love. God "visits" us in the depths of our infirmities. How could this divine "greeting" fail to be "saving"? Christ has compassion; he feels pity; he is deeply moved. God is Love, and in Christ this love takes a human form, is mediated through a human heart, finds expression in human language, in order that it may encounter human beings at the level where they experience their wretchedness and may bring home to them the intensity of God's concern for them.

3. Signs of the Coming of the Messianic Kingdom

Christ's primary activity was to heal the sick and expel demons (Mk 1:35–39). He was unwilling, however, to be taken for a simple healer or to let himself be made prisoner of that kind of image. He made clear the real meaning of these acts of power. His miracles are connected with the theme of the kingdom (Lk 9:11; Mt 10:35); they prolong in the form of action Christ's preaching on the coming of the kingdom. In Jesus of Nazareth the promises are now fulfilled; in him the Messiah is present.[3] For men and women are now healed of their infirmities; they are delivered from sin; and the good news is proclaimed to the poor (Lk 7:22, Is 35:5–6; 26:19). The changed situation which Isaiah prophesied (Is 49:25) is now a reality. The words and actions of Christ are charged with a power that dethrones Satan and inaugurates the reign of God: "If it is by the Spirit of God that I cast out demons, then the kingdom of God has come upon you" (Mt 12:28; Lk 11:20).

In the eyes of Jesus the deliverance of the possessed is no less important than the healing of the sick, for if salvation comes, it is because God, in the person of his envoy, triumphs over the shadowy power of evil and the Evil One. The kingdom of God is not a utopian dream nor a distant presence; it is already here. Healings and exorcisms are two forms of deliverance that manifest and demonstrate that the reign of Satan is being dismantled and that the reign of God is at hand: "I saw Satan fall like lightning from heaven" (Lk 10:17–18). By expelling demons and healing the sick Christ not only signifies that he is breaking the power of Satan; in these actions he really breaks it and effectively establishes the reign of God. Wherever Christ is, the saving and life-giving power that the prophets had foretold is at work; it triumphs over sickness and death, as well as over sin and Satan.[4]

In Christ the power of God is at work, that irrepressible power that is capable of transforming the entire person, body and soul, into the image of Christ. But in order that human beings may realize that the prophecies are fulfilled, that Satan is conquered, and that a new world is present at the heart of the old, Christ *makes visible* the complete salvation which he is proclaiming. He turns human

> *In Christ the power of God is at work, that irrepressible power that is capable of transforming the entire person, body and soul, into the image of Christ.*

beings enslaved by Satan into healthy, justified human beings. His victory over sin, sickness, and death is at the same time a pledge of the new world which he inaugurates by his own resurrection.[5]

Endnotes

1. Vatican I describes miracles as displays of divine omnipotence in the service of revelation: "they manifestly display the omnipotence . . . of God" (DS 3009; Neuner-Dupuis 119).
2. See X. Léon-Dufour (ed.), *Les miracles de Jésus* (Paris, 1977), 213–85; P. Biard, *La Puissance de Dieu* (Paris, 1960); C. Tresmontant, *Études de métaphysique biblique* (Paris, 1955), 223–28; R. Latourelle, "Miracle," *Dictionnaire de spiritualité* 10 (1979) 1274–75.
3. In their Jewish context the miracles thus have a twofold probative value: 1. in virtue of their traditional juridical function; 2. as fulfillments of the Scriptures.
4. On the connection between sickness, death, sin, and Satan see Ph. H. Menoud, "La signification du miracle dans le Nouveau Testament," *Revue d'histoire et de philosophie religieuses* 28–29 (1948–49) 173–92.
5. On this aspect of miracles see especially: C. Dumont, "Unité et diversité des signes de la Révélation," *Nouvelle revue théologique* 80 (1958) 136–37; P. Biard (n. 2), 117–20; L. Monden, *Signs and Wonders. A Study of the Miraculous Element in Religion* (New York, 1966), 36–41; F. Taymans, "Le miracle, signe du surnaturel," *Nouvelle revue théologique* 77 (1955) 230-31; A. George, "Les miracles de Jesus dans les Evangiles synoptiques," *Lumière et vie* no. 33 (1957) 18–20; Ph. H. Menoud (n. 4), 177–81; A. Richardson, *The Miracle Stories of the Gospels* (London, 1956), 38–58; J. Kallas, *The Significance of the Gospel Miracles* (London, 1961), 77–101; R. E. Brown, "The Gospel Miracles," in *The Bible in Current Catholic Thought* (New York, 1986), 190–92; R. Latourelle, *Théologie de la Révélation* (Montreal, 1969), 470–72; idem, "Miracle," *Dictionnaire de spiritualité* 10:1275–76.

For Reflection

1. Latourelle writes that miracles are signs not merely of power, but of power "in the service of love." What is he saying about other kinds of power in contrast with Jesus' power? What are some examples of power *not* at the service of love?

2. The third point in the excerpt explains that the miracles of Jesus point to the coming of the Kingdom. If the miracles show that the Reign of God is present in Jesus, then what are some features of the Kingdom of God?

3. Latourelle explains that Jesus is the Revelation of the Father, showing us what God is like. Which of Jesus' miracles speaks most powerfully to you? What sign value do you think it points to about God?

12 The Eucharist: Blessed Sacrament

Introduction

"For on the night he was betrayed he himself took bread, and, giving you thanks, he said the blessing, broke the bread and gave it to his disciples." These words from Eucharistic Prayer III remind us of how Christ instituted the Sacrament of the Eucharist. Just before the priest speaks these words, he calls upon God to make holy the offering of bread and wine so that they "may become the Body and Blood of your Son our Lord Jesus Christ." Take a minute to think about what it means for the priest to call upon God to turn the bread and wine into the Body and Blood of Christ. The very familiarity of the ritual can cause us to lose sight of the enormity of what is happening at Mass.

In the two meditations in this chapter, Saint John Baptist de La Salle impresses upon his audience—the Brothers of the Christian Schools, the religious organization he founded—the benefits available to those who receive Holy Communion. De La Salle urges all of us to recognize that Jesus is truly present in the Holy Eucharist and that the Eucharist is substantial food for the soul.

Finding Christ in the Old Testament

De La Salle refers to Bible passages that his community would have known. The story of Elias (known to us as Elijah) is one example. Pursued through the desert by assassins, Elijah was so worn out that he lay down and begged God to take his life. An angel brought bread and water, and Elijah found the strength to travel to safety (1 Kings 19:1–8). De La Salle interprets this Old Testament story in light of the Gospel, noting that it prefigures the strengthening effects of the Eucharist.

In the first meditation, De La Salle reminds us that the bread Jesus offers strengthens us spiritually and that sharing in Holy Communion allows us to share in Jesus' very life forever. The wording of the second meditation shifts from "bread" to "meat." This usage may seem odd to us, but recall that Jesus used the term "my flesh" to describe what he offered at the Last Supper when he instituted the Eucharist. Today when we think of bread we may not think of hearty, sustaining food, but the word *meat* certainly evokes that meaning. De La Salle uses the image of meat to reiterate how the Holy Eucharist strengthens us and unites us so closely with Christ that we actually come to share in his divine life.

As the spiritual leader of his congregation, De La Salle intended to challenge the brothers to reflect on their own degrees of faith and commitment by posing questions for them to carry into the period of silent prayer that would have followed the public reading of the *Meditations* in this religious community. Today we can also find in these readings a challenge. In the many questions De La Salle poses about our own attitudes toward the Holy Eucharist, you will find at least one you can take away and ponder.

Excerpts from *Meditations*

By Saint John Baptist de La Salle

Friday in the Octave of the Blessed Sacrament

Jesus Christ in the Holy Eucharist, bread that nourishes our souls

48.1 First Point

The Jews gloried in the fact that Moses had given their forefathers a bread from heaven, but Jesus Christ told them that they were mistaken, that it was his Eternal Father who gives the true bread from heaven and that he is this living Bread come down from heaven (Jn 6:31–32, 51).

Indeed, he is living in those who receive him, for when they receive the sacrament of the holy Eucharist with holy dispositions, he gives himself generously to all the faculties of their souls and carries out there the actions of life. He guides and directs them by his divine Spirit, by whom he lives and acts in them.

When Jesus Christ is in you, is he there as a living bread? Do you allow him complete freedom to communicate his divine Spirit to your soul? Is he living in you to the extent that you can say that it is no longer you who live but that it is Jesus Christ who lives in you (Gal 2:20)?

48.2 Second Point

Jesus Christ told the Jews that he was the true bread come down from heaven. He added that this bread gives life to the world. He says even more that whoever eats this bread will never be hungry (Jn 6:51, 33, 35).

> 66 *Eat this divine bread, then, gladly, with love, and as often as you can.* 99

How fortunate we are to be able to satisfy our hunger with such bread as often as we wish!

This is the bread that nourishes you so well that you find in it all the spiritual sustenance and vigor you need. This is why the Fathers of the Church say that this is the **supersubstantial** bread (Mt 6:11) spoken of in the Lord's prayer according to Saint Matthew. For nothing is better able to sustain our soul and to give it such surpassing strength to walk vigorously in the path of virtue.

The bread that Elias ate before reaching the summit of Mount Horeb, which alone sufficed to strengthen him for his journey of forty days (1 Kgs 19:7–8), is also regarded as a figure of the sacred bread of the Eucharist.

Eat this divine bread, then, gladly, with love, and as often as you can. If you learn how to find in it all the encouragement it contains, it will give your soul a truly heavenly life here on earth.

48.3 Third Point

Seeing that the Jews found it difficult to believe what he was telling them, Jesus Christ added that he was

The Jews Language borrowed from the Gospel of John; used by some authors in previous eras as a general way to identify those who rejected the teachings of Jesus.

supersubstantial More than materially substantial; able to sustain spiritually.

himself the bread of life, that their forefathers who had eaten the manna had all died, but that those who eat of this bread come down from heaven will never die; that if anyone eats of this bread, he will live forever; that this bread which he will give is his own flesh (Jn 6:48–51).

When we receive the body of Jesus Christ, we have the advantage of sharing in our Savior's life, of having in us an assurance of eternal life. We are even guaranteed to live forever if we preserve in ourselves the Spirit of Jesus Christ, which is what he leaves in us.

Is it possible that Jesus Christ promises that you will live with an eternal life by eating this bread, which is God, and that you want either not to eat it or to eat it only rarely? Taste and see (Ps 34:9) how good this bread is for you, how pleasing it is to your taste, and how beneficial for your soul.

Saturday in the Octave of the Blessed Sacrament

Jesus Christ in the Eucharist, food that sustains the life of our souls

49.1 First Point

In the Gospel Jesus Christ calls the Holy Eucharist not only bread but also meat. My flesh, he says, is food (Jn 6:55). As such, it gives the soul a vigor that makes it easy to overcome all the difficulties found in the practice of virtue.

Nothing, in effect, can disturb the soul, because Jesus Christ communicates to it in some manner the energy that can withstand whatever opposes its good. He also gives the soul courage to reassure it against whatever it might fear in the attacks of its enemies.

We even grow stronger, says **Tertullian**, by this flesh, which is why it is more necessary for us to feed upon it to procure for our soul an abundance of grace than to nourish our body with ordinary meat to preserve life.

The more virtue and perfection your **state** demands of you, the more strength and generosity you need to achieve this and not allow yourself to

Tertullian A second-century North African Father of the Church and early Christian writer; some call him the founder of Western theology.

state Condition or stage in life; here it refers to whether one is a priest, a member of a religious order, or a single or married person.

be laid low by fear of the sufferings you will encounter on your way. Nourish yourself with this Eucharistic meat to be strengthened interiorly and to overcome all the obstacles to your salvation.

49.2 Second Point

This divine meat of the Eucharist produces another effect in us; those who eat it live in Jesus Christ, and Jesus Christ lives in them (Jn 6:56). He assures us of this in the holy Gospel. This shows that between Jesus Christ and the person who eats his flesh, such a close and intimate union is brought about that only with difficulty can one be separated from the other. This sacred food is incorporated in the soul that receives it with fervor, so that this soul shares in the virtues of Jesus Christ, and what was said of the spouse in the Canticle takes place: My lover belongs to me, and I belong to my lover (Song 6:3).

Are you thus so closely united to Jesus Christ when you receive him that nothing is able to separate you from him? After receiving Communion, can you say with Saint Paul, Who will separate me from Jesus Christ? Will it be tribulation, poverty, persecution, hunger, nakedness, or danger (Rom 8:35)? Can you add, with all the confidence of the Apostle, that no creature can ever separate you from your Savior (Rom 8:39)? See to it that your holy Communion produces between you and Jesus Christ a union so strong that you will never be separated from him.

49.3 Third Point

Another admirable effect produced in a soul by the divine meat of the Eucharist is that it makes the soul live an altogether supernatural and divine life. This is made clear when Jesus Christ says: As my Father who sent me lives and as I live by my Father, so too the one who eats me will live by me (Jn 6:57).

A soul who eats, then, this flesh of Jesus Christ and is nourished by this meat no longer lives a natural life, no longer seeks to satisfy its senses, no longer acts by its own spirit but by the Spirit of its God, who has become its nourishment.

Are these the effects produced in you by union with Jesus Christ in the Eucharist?

For Reflection

1. De La Salle writes that the Holy Eucharist can give the soul "a truly heavenly life here on earth." What characteristics would you expect to see in someone living that kind of life?

2. The author seems amazed that some people do not want to receive the Eucharist. Why does he seem so surprised by this? What benefits does he think everyone should want to experience?

3. Near the beginning of the Saturday meditation, De La Salle mentions attacks by enemies of the soul. What kind of attacks does he seem to have in mind? Identify some realities—whether internal (within oneself) or external (in the environment)—that young people today may experience as attacks on the soul.

Part 4
Christ, the Redeemer

13 The Jews and the Death of Jesus

Introduction

Every few years a new movie, play, or book drags an age-old question back into the headlines: Did the Jews kill Jesus? In 2010 the question surfaced as the time approached for the world-famous Oberammergau Passion Play, which has been staged in the Bavarian village of Oberammergau every ten years since 1634. The question dominated the news in 2003, with the release of Mel Gibson's movie *The Passion of the Christ*. Some critics claim that any retelling of the events of Jesus' suffering and death will stir up anti-Semitism—that is, hatred or anger against Jews. But many groups, as well as the Catholic Church, have suggested that there are ways to tell the story that steer clear of the dangers of anti-Semitism.

The problem of implicating the Jews in Jesus' death began in the conflict between the earliest followers of Jesus and their Jewish neighbors who did not follow Jesus. That conflict worked its way into the retelling of events in Jesus' life, especially the events surrounding his Passion. Because the Gospels and the Epistles emerged from the earliest Christian communities, they reflect the life and times of those early believers.

Oberammergau

The residents of Oberammergau, a small village in Germany, have performed a Passion play every ten years since 1634, having promised the year before to do so if God would spare them from destruction by the bubonic plague. In 2010 nearly half the inhabitants of the village reportedly took part in the play. Partly in response to the Second Vatican Council, a creative team continues to revise the play. Those who attend in 2020 will notice that Jesus prays in Hebrew and that he is addressed as "Rabbi."

For centuries afterward it was not unusual to hear Christian preachers blame the Jewish people for killing Jesus, fueling prejudice against people whose religious beliefs and practices already set them apart from their neighbors in predominantly Christian communities. That kind of preaching—whether it reflected simple ignorance or outright malice—provided a ready excuse for anyone who wished to strip the Jews of their rights and property. Even as recently as the last two centuries, during the organized massacres of European Jews known as pogroms, attackers often shouted the hateful accusation. And we cannot forget that the pogroms culminated in the Holocaust—in Hebrew called the *Shoah*.

But were the Jews in fact responsible for Jesus' death? Scholars tell us that it was the Romans who executed Jesus, using the Roman method of crucifixion. It is true that the Jewish authorities did find Jesus guilty of a capital crime, and according to the Gospels many in Jerusalem called for his death. But in considering the question of who is responsible, the *United States Catholic Catechism for Adults* answers this way: "Every one of us from the dawn of history to the end of time who in pride and disobedience has sinned is in some way responsible. . . . It is wrong to blame the Jewish people for the death of Christ in the manner that often has been done in history" (p. 92).

As we have seen, the misconception about the culpability of Jews in the death of Jesus has given rise to centuries of Western anti-Semitism. We can glimpse this legacy through the excerpts here—two modern attempts to address and even heal those wounds. In the first excerpt, from the 1965 *Declaration on the Relation of the Church to Non-Christian Religions* (*Nostra Aetate*), the Second Vatican Council clarifies the Church's teachings about the Jewish people. The Council explains that although certain Jews in Jerusalem bore some responsibility for Jesus' death, there is no foundation for blaming the entire Jewish populace for Jesus' death, and certainly no basis for blaming modern-day Jews. The *Declaration on the Relation of the Church to Non-Christian Religions* helped to open the Church to respectful dialogue with other faiths, including Judaism.

The second excerpt is from *God's Mercy Endures Forever: Guidelines on the Presentation of Jews and Judaism in Catholic Preaching,* from the Committee on the Liturgy of the **National Conference of Catholic Bishops**. The full document aims to help **homilists** present the Jewish people in a way that is consistent with Church teaching. This second reading builds on the reading from Vatican Council II, reminding us that the message of Christ's Passion is not about who is responsible. In fact, whenever Christians have held the Jewish people responsible for Christ's death, the bishops tell us, they have drawn "themselves away from the paschal mystery" (22). The Gospel accounts of Christ's Passion, death, and Resurrection reveal his profound and abiding love for us, no matter what sins we may have committed. Rather than looking for someone to blame, we are called to turn away from sin so "that we can hope to rise with Christ to new life" (22).

Misreading or deliberately misapplying the words of Scripture has led to accusations against the Jews and anti-Semitism for centuries. But the second reading in this chapter suggests another consequence. Placing the blame on others relieves us of the responsibility to look into our own hearts. If we focus on the question of who killed Jesus, we avoid more difficult questions: Do I believe that Jesus is the true Son of God, or not? Have I rejected Jesus in my words or actions? In what ways do I contribute to Jesus' Passion through my words and actions? These are the deeper questions the Crucifixion narratives present to us.

National Conference of Catholic Bishops The former name of the United States Conference of Catholic Bishops. Each country or region has its own conference of bishops supporting the work of the Church in that part of the world.

homilists Those who write and deliver homilies, that is, bishops, priests, and deacons.

Excerpt from *Declaration on the Relation of the Church to Non-Christian Religions (Nostra Aetate)*

By the Second Vatican Council

4. As the sacred synod searches into the mystery of the Church, it remembers the bond that spiritually ties the people of the New Covenant to Abraham's stock.

Thus the Church of Christ acknowledges that, according to God's saving design, the beginnings of her faith and her election are found already among the Patriarchs, Moses and the prophets. She professes that all who believe in Christ—Abraham's sons according to faith (cf. *Gal.* 3:7)—are included in the same Patriarch's call, and likewise that the salvation of the Church is mysteriously foreshadowed by the chosen people's exodus from the land of bondage. The Church, therefore, cannot forget that she received the revelation of the Old Testament through the people with whom God in His inexpressible mercy concluded the Ancient Covenant. Nor can she forget that she draws sustenance from the root of that well-cultivated olive tree onto which have been grafted the wild shoots, the Gentiles (cf. *Rom.* 11:17–24). Indeed, the Church believes that by His cross Christ, Our Peace, reconciled Jews and Gentiles, making both one in Himself (cf. *Eph.* 2:14–16).

The Church keeps ever in mind the words of the Apostle about his kinsmen: "theirs is the sonship and the glory and the covenants and the law and the worship and the promises; theirs are the fathers and from them is the Christ according to the flesh" (*Rom.* 9:4–5), the Son of the Virgin Mary. She also recalls that the Apostles, the Church's main-stay and pillars, as well as most of the early disciples who proclaimed Christ's Gospel to the world, sprang from the Jewish people.

As Holy Scripture testifies, Jerusalem did not recognize the time of her visitation [by the Son of God] (cf. *Lk.* 19:44), nor did the Jews in large number, accept the Gospel; indeed not a few opposed its spreading (cf. *Rom.* 11:28). Nevertheless, God holds the Jews most dear for the sake of their Fathers; He does not repent of the gifts He makes or of the calls He issues—such is the witness of the Apostle [Paul] (cf. *Rom.* 11:28–29).[1] In company with the Prophets and the same Apostle, the Church awaits that day, known to God alone, on which all peoples will address the Lord in a single voice and "serve him shoulder to shoulder" (*Soph.* 3:9; cf. *Is.* 66:23; *Ps.* 65:4; *Rom.* 11:11–32).

> ❝ *Christ underwent His passion and death freely, because of the sins of men and out of infinite love, in order that all may reach salvation.* ❞

Since the spiritual **patrimony** common to Christians and Jews is thus so great, this sacred synod [the Second Vatican Council] wants to foster and recommend that mutual understanding and respect which is the fruit, above all, of biblical and theological studies as well as of fraternal dialogues.

True, the Jewish authorities and those who followed their lead pressed for the death of Christ (cf. *John* 19:6); still, what happened in His passion cannot be charged against all the Jews, without distinction, then alive, nor against the Jews of today. Although the Church is the new people of God, the Jews should not be presented as rejected or accursed by God, as if this followed from the Holy Scriptures. All should see to it, then, that in catechetical work or in the preaching of the word of God they do not teach anything that does not conform to the truth of the Gospel and the spirit of Christ.

Furthermore, in her rejection of every persecution against any man, the Church, mindful of the patrimony she shares with the Jews and moved not by political reasons but by the Gospel's spiritual love, decries hatred, persecutions, displays of anti-Semitism, directed against Jews at any time and by anyone.

Besides, as the Church has always held and holds now, Christ underwent His passion and death freely, because of the sins of men and out of infinite love, in order that all may reach salvation. It is, therefore, the burden of the Church's preaching to

patrimony An inheritance from God the Father.

proclaim the cross of Christ as the sign of God's all-embracing love and as the fountain from which every grace flows.

Endnote

1. Cf. Dogmatic Constitution, *Lumen Gentium* (Light of nations) AAS, 57 (1965) page 20.

Excerpt from *God's Mercy Endures Forever: Guidelines on the Presentation of Jews and Judaism in Catholic Preaching*

By the Bishops' Committee on the Liturgy, National Conference of Catholic Bishops

Historical Perspectives and Contemporary Proclamation

7. Another misunderstanding rejected by the Second Vatican Council was the notion of collective guilt, which charged the Jewish people *as a whole* with responsibility for Jesus' death. . . . From the theory of collective guilt, it followed for some that Jewish suffering over the ages reflected divine retribution on the Jews for an alleged "**deicide**." While both rabbinic Judaism and early Christianity saw in the destruction of the Jerusalem Temple in A.D. 70 a sense of divine punishment (see Lk 19:42–44), the theory of collective guilt went well beyond Jesus' poignant expression of his love as a Jew for Jerusalem and the destruction it would face at the hands of Imperial Rome. Collective guilt implied that because "the Jews" had rejected Jesus, God had rejected them. With direct reference to Luke 19:44, the Second Vatican Council reminded Catholics that "nevertheless, now as before, God holds the Jews most dear for the sake of their fathers; he does not repent of the gifts he makes or of the calls he issues," and established . . . that "the Jews should not be represented as rejected by God or accursed, as if this followed from Holy Scripture" (*Nostra Aetate*, no. 4; cf. 1985 *Notes [on the Correct Way to Present the Jews and Judaism in Preaching and Catechesis of the Roman Catholic Church]*, VI:33). . . .

deicide The act of killing God.

Holy Week: The Passion Narratives

. . . 22. The message of the liturgy in proclaiming the passion narratives in full is to enable the assembly to see vividly the love of Christ for each person, despite their sins, a love that even death could not vanquish. "Christ in his boundless love freely underwent his passion and death because of the sins of all so that all might attain salvation" (*Nostra Aetate*, no. 4). To the extent that Christians over the centuries made Jews the scapegoat for Christ's death, they drew themselves away from the paschal mystery. For it is only by dying to one's sins that we can hope to rise with Christ to new life. This is a central truth of the Catholic faith stated by the *Catechism* of the Council of Trent in the sixteenth century and reaffirmed by the 1985 *Notes* (no. 30).

For Reflection

1.   Based on what you have read in this chapter's selections, how would you respond to a student who, during a class discussion of the Crucifixion narratives, says that the Jews killed Jesus? What might you say to explain the Church's teaching about the role of the Jews in Jesus' Passion and death?

2.   The first excerpt, from Vatican Council II, names some of the Church's connections to Judaism. Choose one and explain it in your own words.

3.   What reasons does the Council give for directing that the Jews should not be "presented as rejected or accursed by God"?

4.   The second excerpt says that when we look for someone to blame for Christ's death, we turn "away from the paschal mystery." In your own words, explain why this is so. What was the purpose of Jesus' suffering and death?

14 Grounds for Belief in the Resurrection

Introduction

How do we know the Resurrection really happened? No one today can prove it, but we can offer evidence for the truth of the biblical claim that Jesus rose from the dead. That is precisely what Archbishop Fulton J. Sheen sets out to do in this excerpt from his 1934 book on the life of Christ, titled *The Eternal Galilean*.

Sheen is well respected as a Catholic apologist. In the language of philosophy, an apologist does not express regret for something; rather, he or she offers arguments to defend controversial ideas. Sheen was particularly well suited for this role. A brilliant scholar who taught philosophy and theology at the Catholic University of America, he wrote hundreds of books and pamphlets on the Catholic faith. He also developed a popular radio program that ran for two decades. He then became the first Catholic preacher on television, even winning an Emmy in 1952. As a teacher, author, and media personality, he was unusually able to appeal to a broad audience, from theologians to any Catholic with a radio or television.

In this excerpt, Sheen uses language that is easy to follow to explain why we should believe in the Resurrection. He argues against the notion that the Apostles experienced a shared delusion or that the Resurrection accounts are the results of hallucination. Using evidence from the Gospels to show that Jesus' followers were caught completely off guard by the events following his death, Sheen argues that only the most convincing physical evidence could have led them to proclaim the Risen Savior. Sheen also offers as evidence the tremendous change in the disciples' behavior. Only some mysterious power, he suggests, could have brought about such a remarkable transformation.

The excerpt ends with Sheen's conviction that the eyewitnesses to the Resurrection were not the only ones transformed by an astoundingly powerful event. The Resurrection transformed—and continues to transform—all of us who have followed in the footsteps of those early believers.

Excerpt from *The Eternal Galilean*
By Archbishop Fulton J. Sheen

The Resurrection was a fact. He said He would rise again. And He did rise again! *Resurrexit sicut dixit*! Oh! Think not that Peter and the Apostles were the victims of a delusion; think not they had an hallucination and mistook their subjective ideas for the manifestation of the Conqueror of Death. All those who saw the One Whom they thought dead walk in the newness of life had to be convinced. They were not even expecting the Resurrection. The absence of the Apostles at the crucifixion . . . prove[s] they thought Death ended all. On Easter morning the women went to the sepulcher not to meet the Risen Christ, but to embalm the body; their greatest worry was who would roll away the stone from the door of the sepulcher; even when they found it rolled away, they did not suppose a resurrection but only a shameful theft of the body. The message of the angel inspires them not with faith, but with fear and horror.

The Apostles had the same state of mind—the one thing they were afraid of was an hallucination. Hence when the women announced the Resurrection, instead of being impressed they regarded the words of women as "idle tales and believed them not"; Peter and John verified the empty tomb but still knew not the Scriptures concerning the Resurrection. Why, they were so far away from the idea of seeing Him upset the human concept of Death, that when they first saw Him, they thought they had seen

Resurrexit sicut dixit Latin for Matthew 28:6: "He has been raised just as he said."

Emmaus A village near Jerusalem. Luke 24:13–35 tells the story of two travelers who encountered the Risen Christ on the road to this city.

a ghost; Mary Magdalene thought He was the gardener, and the disciples on the way to **Emmaus** did not recognize Him until the breaking of bread, and when they told the other disciples, they were not believed. When He appeared in Galilee, Matthew tells us that some doubted. The very evening of the Resurrection some of His Apostles would not even believe their own eyes until they saw Him eating. Thomas even then doubted and would not be convinced until he put finger unto His Hand, and his hand into the Divine Side to be cured of his doubt and [be] made the Hope and Healer of Agnostics until the end of time.

If His followers were expecting Him, they would have believed at once. If they did finally believe, it was only because the sheer weight of external evidence was too strong to resist. They had to be convinced, and they were convinced. They had to admit their views on death were wrong—Christ was not dead. Life then does not mean what men call life. Hence the world and its ideas had to be remade—for here was a force greater than Nature! Nature had not finished her accounting with Him for Nature received the only serious blow it ever received—the mortal wound of an empty tomb; enemies had not finished their accounting with Him, for they who slew the foe found they had lost their day. Humanity has not finished its accounting, for He came from a grave to show the breast where a Roman spear had forever made visible the Heart, which loved men enough to die for them, and then live on in order to love forever; the human mind has not finished its last accounting, for it now has to learn that what men call life is only death, that bodily life is not true life, that he who gives up his soul ruins also the flesh which houses it—in a word, *it was not Christ who died; it was Death.*

> ❝ *Think for the moment on the conduct of the Apostles before the Resurrection, and the way they acted when the Spirit gave them the fullness of belief in the Risen Saviour.* ❞

Think for the moment on the conduct of the Apostles before the Resurrection, and the way they acted when the Spirit gave them the fullness of belief in the Risen Saviour. What new force so transformed the souls of the Apostles, so as to make the abject, the venerated; the ignorant, masters; the egotists, the devoted; and the despairing, saints? What power was it that laid hold of Peter who once said he knew not the Man, and now before a

> **Pentecost**
>
> In the excerpt here, when Sheen mentions that the Spirit gave the Apostles "the fullness of belief in the Risen Saviour," he is referring to Pentecost. The second chapter of the Acts of the Apostles relates the story: After the Holy Spirit came to rest on each of Jesus' followers who had gathered that day, Peter preached the Good News to the crowds. People from all over the world understood Peter's words as if he were speaking their own language.

learned audience of Parthians and Medes and Elamites, of Mesopotamians, Phrygians and Egyptians and Romans, arises to startle their hearts and thrill their souls with the message, "You have killed the Author of Life. Do penance and be baptized every one of you in the name of Jesus Christ for the remission of sins." What hand was it that laid hold of Saul, the bitter enemy of Christians, converted him into a Paul and the preacher who counted all things as naught save the glory of the Risen Christ? What new spirit entered into that crude, fish-smelling group of Galilean fishermen which compelled them to go to the capital of the world, which brushed them aside with disdain, and there preach the seemingly grotesque creed that He who was executed as a common criminal by a Roman Procurator was the Resurrection and the Life? . . . Some new dynamics, some new colossal power had to enter into such simple souls to disrupt a Jewish world and impress itself in twenty years on the entire shore of the Mediterranean from Caesarea to Troas. There is only one force in the world which explains how habitual doubters, like Thomas, sensitive tax-gatherers like Matthew, dull men like Philip, impetuous characters like Peter, gentle dreamers like John, and a few seafaring men reeling under the shock of a crucifixion, could be transformed into men of fire, ready to suffer, dare, and if need be to die—and that is the force of love which showed itself in the Christ Whom the builders rejected, and who now was made the head of the corner. Everywhere, they gave the secret of their success: they were witnesses of a Resurrection; He who was dead, liveth. And eleven of them went out to have their throats cut in testimony of that belief—and men generally do not have their throats cut for an hallucination. There was only one conclusion their blood will let us draw and that is the lesson of Easter Day which they preached—*It was not Christ who died; it was Death.*

The cycles of the years whirl away into history, but it was ever the same antiphon that went up from the hearts of men. Each age repeated it in its own way so that no generation of men was without the tidings of victory. See how that lesson was verified as the followers of the Risen Christ taught Rome the real reason why it was eternal. Hardly grown to their full stature, **Nero** published his famous edict: "Let there be no Christians," and his successors, with no fear of God to restrain their cruelty, and a great army to administer it, set to work to destroy the Gospel of the Risen Saviour. The swords of the executioners, blunted with slaughter, no longer fitted their sheaths; the wild beasts satiated with Christian blood shrank from it as if more conscious of its dignity than those who ordered it spilt; the river of the Tiber ran red as if already one of the angels of the Apocalypse had poured into it the vial which turns water into blood. From a thousand times a thousand throats there came the cry: "The Christians must die," as a thousand times a thousand thumbs turned down in signal of death. A day finally came when Rome thought it had cut off the last hand that would make the sign of the Cross and silenced the last tongue that would breathe the name of the risen Christ—and yet what is the verdict of history? The verdict of history is the verdict of the empty tomb. It was the same antiphon struck on a different key. It was not the Christians who died. It was the Roman Empire. *It was not Christ who died; it was Death.*

Nero A first-century Roman emperor.

For Reflection

1. What evidence does Sheen give to demonstrate that the followers of Jesus were not expecting the Resurrection?

2. How does Sheen describe the transformation seen in Jesus' Apostles, which he attributes to their encounters with the Risen Christ?

3. In the discussion that follows this passage in his book, Sheen goes on to relate the story of heroic Christian faith in his own time, the early twentieth century. In what ways do we need courage and faith to be Christians in twenty-first–century America?

15 Why Christ Was Raised

Introduction

You probably know that *Gospel* means "good news." But could you summarize the Good News in a nutshell? One of the earliest summaries of the Gospel is recounted by Saint Paul in First Corinthians: "For I handed on to you as of first importance what I also received: that Christ died for our sins in accordance with the scriptures; that he was buried; that he was raised on the third day in accordance with the scriptures; that he appeared to Cephas, then to the Twelve" (15:3–5). These facts are the very foundation of our faith.

In this chapter two early Church Fathers, Saint Maximus of Turin and Saint Leo the Great, explain the significance of the Resurrection. The two readings are excerpts from sermons they preached sometime during the fifth century, the closing days of the Roman Empire.

Saint Maximus, a biblical scholar and bishop of Turin, echoes Saint Paul in proclaiming, "Christ is this day." He builds on a passage in the Gospel of John, which identifies Christ as the light of the human race: "the light shines in the darkness, / and the darkness has not overcome it" (1:5). The contrast of darkness and light is an important theme in John's Gospel: Humanity is caught in a cosmic battle between light and darkness; Jesus is the true light of the world, enlightening believers by reveal-

> **Church Fathers**
>
> In the Church the term *father* means "a teacher of spiritual things." Some teachers and writers of the early Church, many of whom were bishops, are called Church Fathers. Their teachings witness to the apostolic Tradition.

ing God; Christians are called to embrace the light. This metaphor of Christ as the light would have been familiar to those hearing these sermons. The concept was so well understood that in the fifth-century baptismal **liturgy**, when the candidates renounced the devil, they turned to the East to face the light. The newly baptized were even called *neophytes*, meaning the newly enlightened—a term we still use today in the Rite of Christian Initiation for Adults. Building on his audience's knowledge of this powerful symbol, Saint Maximus contrasts the light of Christ with the darkness of sin. The significance of the Resurrection is that Christ, the light, has finally and for all time overcome the darkness of sin in the world. When Maximus says, "No sin can overshadow the justice of Christ," he means there is no sin for which a believer in Christ cannot be forgiven.

Saint Leo the Great was Pope in the mid-fifth century. The Church recognizes Leo's significant contribution to Church teaching by naming him one of thirty-three Doctors of the Church, saints who are highly esteemed for their contributions to the Church's learning. In his sermon excerpt in this chapter, he preaches on the period between Jesus' Resurrection and his Ascension into Heaven. He sums up the events of those forty days: Christ removed the fear of death, filled the Apostles with the Holy Spirit, and made Peter our first Pope by entrusting to him the care of the Church. Saint Leo is a master of understatement when he says those days "were by no means uneventful."

Why did Christ stay with his disciples for forty days? Saint Leo explains that during that time, the Risen Christ strengthened their faith and convinced them beyond doubt that his Resurrection was a fact. The disciples' great joy at the Ascension shows that they did come to believe it, as Leo points out; otherwise, they would have been sad to see their beloved teacher leave.

Leo points to another source of joy for us as followers of Jesus: our own

> **liturgy** The Church's official, public, communal prayer. It is God's work, in which the People of God participate.

glorified humanity. Human nature itself, once so damaged by the Fall, gained new dignity in Christ's Resurrection and Ascension. Because the Risen Christ embodied both the divine and the human, when he is glorified in heaven, so also is our own humanity.

In the readings in this chapter, Saints Maximus and Leo offer several reasons for rejoicing in Christ's Resurrection. They challenge us to consider why we might rejoice when we hear the Good News about the Risen Christ.

Excerpt from a Sermon, "Christ Is the Day"
By Saint Maximus of Turin

Christ is risen! He has burst open the gates of hell and let the dead go free; he has renewed the earth through the members of his Church now born again in baptism, and has made it blossom afresh with men brought back to life. His Holy Spirit has unlocked the doors of heaven, which stand wide open to receive those who rise up from the earth. Because of Christ's resurrection the thief ascends to paradise, the bodies of the blessed enter the holy city, and the dead are restored to the company of the living. There is an upward movement in the whole of creation, each element raising itself to something higher. We see hell restoring its victims to the upper regions, earth sending its buried dead to heaven, and heaven presenting the new arrivals to the Lord. In one and the same movement, our Savior's passion raises men from the depths, lifts them up from the earth, and sets them in the heights.

Public Penance

In the fifth century, the Sacrament of Reconciliation was different from what we know today. Then the Church forgave serious sins only once in a lifetime. Those guilty of serious sin usually confessed in front of the community. Afterward, like those preparing for Baptism, the penitents underwent a forty-day purification before the Easter Vigil, during which time they were not admitted to the Eucharistic meal but simply fasted and devoted themselves to prayer. Depending on the sin, penance could last for years.

Christ is risen. His rising brings life to the dead, forgiveness to sinners, and glory to the saints. And so David the prophet summons all creation to join in celebrating the Easter festival: *Rejoice and be glad,* he cries, *on this day which the Lord has made.*

The light of Christ is an endless day that knows no night. Christ is this day, says the Apostle [Paul]; such is the meaning of his words: *Night is almost over; day is at hand.* He tells us that night is almost over, not that it is about to fall. By this we are meant to understand that the coming of Christ's light puts Satan's darkness to flight, leaving no place for any shadow of sin. His everlasting radiance dispels the dark clouds of the past and checks the hidden growth of vice. The Son is that day to whom the day, which is the Father, communicates the mystery of his divinity. He is the day

> " *His rising brings life to the dead, forgiveness to sinners, and glory to the saints.* "

who says through the mouth of Solomon: *I have caused an unfailing light to rise in heaven.* And as in heaven no night can follow day, so no sin can overshadow the justice of Christ. The **celestial** day is perpetually bright and shining with brilliant light; clouds can never darken its skies. In the same way, the light of Christ is eternally glowing with luminous radiance and can never be extinguished by the darkness of sin. This is why John the evangelist says: *The light shines in the darkness, and the darkness has never been able to overpower it.*

And so, my brothers, each of us ought surely to rejoice on this holy day. Let no one, conscious of his sinfulness, withdraw from our common celebration, nor let anyone be kept away from our public prayer by the burden of his guilt. Sinner he may indeed be, but he must not despair of pardon on this day which is so highly privileged; for if a thief could receive the grace of paradise, how could a Christian be refused forgiveness?

celestial Heavenly.

Excerpt from a Sermon, "The Days Between the Resurrection and Ascension of Our Lord"

By Saint Leo the Great

Beloved, the days which passed between the Lord's resurrection and his ascension were by no means uneventful; during them great sacramental mysteries were confirmed, great truths revealed. In those days the fear of death with all its horrors was taken away, and the immortality of both body and soul affirmed. It was then that the Lord breathed on all his apostles and filled them with the Holy Spirit; and after giving the keys of the kingdom to blessed Peter, whom he had chosen and set above all the others, he entrusted him with the care of his flock.

During these days the Lord joined two of his disciples as **their companion on the road**, and by chiding them for their timidity and hesitant fears he swept away all the clouds of our uncertainty. Their lukewarm hearts were fired by the light of faith and began to burn within them as the Lord opened up the Scriptures. And as they shared their meal with him, their eyes were opened in the breaking of bread, opened far more happily to the sight of their own glorified humanity than were the eyes of our first parents to the shame of their sin.

Throughout the whole period between the resurrection and ascension, God's providence was at work to instill this one lesson into the hearts of the disciples, to set this one truth before their eyes, that our Lord Jesus Christ, who was truly born, truly suffered and truly died, should be recognized as truly risen from the dead. The blessed apostles together with all the others had been intimidated by the catastrophe of the cross, and their faith in the resurrection had been uncertain; but now they were so strengthened by the evident truth that when their Lord ascended into heaven, far from feeling any sadness, they were filled with great joy.

Indeed that blessed company had a great and inex-

their companion on the road A reference to Luke 24:13–35, the story of two disciples who encountered the Risen Christ on the road to Emmaus.

pressible cause for joy when it saw man's nature rising above the dignity of the whole heavenly creation, above the ranks of angels, above the exalted status of archangels. Nor would there be any limit to its upward course until humanity was admitted to a seat at the right hand of the eternal Father, to be enthroned at last in the glory of him to whose nature it was wedded in the person of the Son.

For Reflection

1. What are some effects of Christ's light that Saint Maximus names? According to Saint Maximus, what does Saint Paul mean when he says that night is almost over?

2. Saint Maximus conveys some good news for those who have sinned. What is that good news? How does his message take on new significance in light of the fifth-century practice of public penance, as described in the sidebar?

3. According to Saint Leo, what truth was God teaching the disciples during the days between the Resurrection and Ascension?

4. What does Saint Leo describe as the final stage of God's saving work on behalf of humanity?

16 Pentecost: Outpouring of the Holy Spirit

Introduction

An Old Testament Feast

Pentecost, meaning "fiftieth day," is fifty days after Easter—but its origin is older. In the Greek-speaking world of the first century, the Jewish feast of Weeks—which the disciples were celebrating when the Holy Spirit descended—was called Pentecost. It recalled how Moses received the Ten Commandments fifty days after the flight from Egypt. The Exodus and the Resurrection both led to freedom. In the Old Testament, God freed his people from slavery and gave laws to guide them; in the New Testament, God freed his people from sin and sent his Spirit to guide us all.

Pentecost In Scripture the event in which the early followers of Jesus received the Holy Spirit. Today the Church celebrates this event on Pentecost Sunday, which occurs seven weeks after Easter Sunday.

Does God make his presence known in our daily lives? Believers would say yes. Those who are aware of the Holy Spirit acting in our day-to-day existence not only believe but also pay attention. The readings in this chapter illustrate how the Holy Spirit works in our lives. The Spirit not only makes God's presence known, but it also empowers us to help build God's Kingdom on earth.

The first selection in this chapter is the account of **Pentecost** found in the Acts of the Apostles, which Luke wrote as a sort of sequel to his Gospel. At the end of Luke's Gospel, Jesus directs his followers to stay in Jerusalem until they are "clothed with power from on high" (Luke 24:49). Jesus then ascends into Heaven. His followers must have been mystified by this cryptic reference to what was in store for them, but they remain in the city. Then on the day of Pentecost, Jesus' meaning becomes clear. His followers are indeed clothed with power, a power that enables them to share the Good News about Christ's saving work in a most surprising way.

In the second excerpt here, from *May I Have This Dance?* Joyce Rupp invites readers today to pay attention to the presence of the Holy Spirit in daily life. Rupp, a well-known spiritual writer active in the Church today, provides examples of how God's Spirit gives us new energy for action. She considers the transformation the disciples experienced and goes on to describe modern-day transformative moments, showing that God continues to send the Spirit into our lives today.

Rupp tells us about moments where the Spirit of God seems to rush into someone's heart, so that the person feels overcome by strong emotions of compassion, gratitude, or awe. But the experience of God's Spirit is not about an emotional high. The account in the Acts of the Apostles makes this clear: Each gift of the Spirit, each experience of God's presence, pushes us to live a life that contributes to God's work by helping to build his Kingdom on earth.

Acts of the Apostles 2:1–11

When the time for Pentecost was fulfilled, they were all in one place together.

And suddenly there came from the sky a noise like a strong driving wind, and it filled the entire house in which they were. Then there appeared to them tongues as of fire, which parted and came to rest on each one of them. And they were all filled with the holy Spirit and began to speak in different tongues, as the Spirit enabled them to proclaim.

Now there were devout Jews from every nation under heaven staying in Jerusalem. At this sound, they gathered in a large crowd, but they were confused because each one heard them speaking in his own language. They were astounded, and in amazement they asked, "Are not all these people who are speaking Galileans? Then how does each of us hear them in his own native language? We are Parthians, Medes, and Elamites, inhabitants of Mesopotamia, Judea and Cappadocia, Pontus and Asia, Phrygia and Pamphylia, Egypt and the districts of Libya near Cyrene, as well as travelers from Rome, both Jews and converts to Judaism, Cretans and Arabs, yet we hear them speaking in our own tongues of the mighty acts of God."

Excerpt from *May I Have This Dance?*
By Joyce Rupp, OSM

In the dark of night, a man came to visit Jesus. This man's fears kept him from seeking Jesus in the daylight, but his burning issues needed to be addressed. As Jesus listened and answered the questions of Nicodemus, he used the wind to describe the Spirit of God: "The wind blows where it pleases; you can hear its sound, but you cannot tell where it comes from or where it is going" (Jn 3:8).

This image reminds me of a mystery I've noticed as I hiked in the Colorado Rockies. The forest can be so still and silent; then suddenly a whoosh of wind sways the trees and whispers across the hills. This is unpredictable and oftentimes when the wind is strong it brings quick changes in the weather. One never knows when this rushing force will come moving through the pines and aspens, bringing a rain or snow storm, but a good hiker is always attentive to its movement.

Pentecost is a feast of the mysterious movement of God. Each year it is an invitation to be attentive once more to God's presence in our lives. The Spirit of God came as unexpectedly as a wind in the mountains upon the followers of Jesus. A rushing wind created life-changing effects in them. In that **Upper Room**, people who had been terrorized with their own fears suddenly experienced an immense freedom and a deep sense of God's life within them. It was uncontrolled and unplanned, the last thing their sad and

upper room Traditional name for the room where Jesus celebrated the Last Supper and where the disciples gathered when they were in Jerusalem. Many believe this was the site of Pentecost as well.

fearful hearts ever expected. With the rushing wind came a surge of courageous energy that hadn't been there before.

In the chaos, the Spirit of God came with an energy beyond their boldest imagination. This coming changed their attitudes and motivated them with enthusiasm and hope. They moved from being weak and discouraged to being people with inner vitality. They discovered a dynamic power of love and a new determination to live what Jesus had proclaimed to them.

We need to stay attuned to the movement of the Spirit if we are to hear the call to transformation or deeper growth. My Pentecosts are rarely large, powerful gales; rather, they are usually little gusts that change my life a little at a time. Like the rushing wind of Pentecost, however, they have been unpredictable and unexpected.

I can forget or take for granted the smaller breezes if I am not deliberately attentive to them. It is easy to dismiss these moments of transformation, either because I am too busy or because I do not recognize the activity of the Divine. Now I keep a daily journal where I record my experiences of the rushing wind.

For example, I have a photo of a homeless woman to remind me of an unexpected moment when the Spirit of God visited me. One day I went to the mailbox and among the envelopes was the latest issue of *Common Boundary* magazine (Sept/Oct, 1991). I sat down to read my correspondence but I felt drawn to the cover of the magazine, a photo of a homeless woman named Esther. I gazed at her wrinkled face,

> **Pentecost is a feast of the mysterious movement of God.**

the open sore on her nose, and the matted stocking cap on her head. But what most caught my attention was the vibrant light in her deep blue eyes. I sat for a long time looking at Esther. As I did so, a gush of tears came. They were tears of compassion for the tremendous pain of the homeless and the resilience that shone in this woman's eyes. They were also the tears of conversion as I realized how little I had really done to change the situation of those who needed shelter. At that moment the rushing wind was calling me to action, calling me to become more directly involved with the poor.

Another time, the rushing wind surprised me on a day I spent in solitude in the woods. I had come there much in need of renewal and refreshment for my spirit. I was disappointed when I did not feel a sense of closeness to God. It was a restless day, void of any significant insights or stirrings of growth. That evening I sat outdoors for a while and watched the cloudy sky. All was quiet and still. As the night cooled I finally went indoors.

An hour later something drew me to the window. Suddenly I saw a most wondrous sight: in the darkness the center of the silver poplar tree was filled with radiant light. It looked as though the heart of the tree was ablaze. Then just beyond the tree, I saw a huge, golden harvest moon coming over the horizon. It had been freed of the dark clouds and its brilliant, round circle of light shone through the branches of the large tree.

I stood amazed by the beauty of the moment. It brought me a profound message: "Wait on God in trust. Continue to live contemplatively for God is with you. What is hidden will be revealed in its own time." How grateful I was for the energy of the rushing wind that moved me to the window.

Often others tell me of their experiences of the Spirit of God energizing their lives. A woman told me she had taken home a church bulletin. In it was the quote: "The light shall never be overcome by the darkness." She felt drawn to that quote and placed it on her refrigerator door. The next day she went to the doctor for a physical and discovered that she had a tumor in her breast. She told me that the quote she had saved was her greatest strength in the days to come. Even as she went for surgery she felt the light within her overcoming the darkness. A little gush of rushing wind had given her courage to face a great difficulty in her life. When she learned the wonderful news that her tumor was benign she felt deep gratitude for the inner strength she had received from finding that simple quote.

The rushing wind often sweeps through our inner space when we try to control an uncomfortable situation. Often these are the very places where we need the energy of the Spirit of God. These times can lead to moments of surrender or to great vulnerability. In our struggles, our defenses tumble down, our walls crack, and our hearts can be penetrated.

Our minds and hearts are opened and the rushing wind offers us the possibility of transformation.

I remember one such moment because it was so surprising and strengthening. It happened while I was giving a retreat to a group of ministers. One of them had come in to talk with me about his spiritual journey. From our past conversations I knew he was keenly aware that his spiritual life was mainly an intellectual one, that he felt safe and secure when he kept his faith in his head. He didn't allow his feelings or his intuition to have much effect on his spiritual growth. He realized this and knew that he needed to experience God in his heart as well. But he held tightly to his intellectual approach for the control it offered—no surprises, no chaos. During the retreat he struggled with letting go and surrendering to God.

When we met for our conference the minister spoke of his meditation on Romans 5:5: "God's love has been poured into our hearts through the Holy Spirit that has been given to us" (NRSV). As he described being astounded at the generosity of God's goodness, he paused and took a deep breath. Suddenly the reality of God's goodness touched his heart. It was a complete surprise to him. I heard him exclaim, "Ah!" Then he sat quietly and tears began streaming down his cheeks. The rushing wind had penetrated his heart and he was overcome with the power of God's abundant love. I waited with him quietly while he continued to weep in joy and awe at the astounding power of God. It was a very profound moment for both of us. I thought to myself: "I have just witnessed an Upper Room event. The rushing wind has swept through this man's heart and filled him with a deep perception of God's bounteous love."

After he left the room I continued to ponder the movement of the Spirit of God. The rushing wind in this man's spirit had been quiet, intense, and transforming. It had penetrated his strong control. I thought about the passage he had been praying, which describes God's love being poured into us. I like the word "poured." Scripture doesn't say that God's love trickles, or is given drop by drop. No, God's love is poured generously into our hearts. There's an abundance about it and a vibrancy like the fullness of rushing wind. This love is lavish and unending, a continuous stream of goodness waiting to fill our spirits with spiritual vitality.

The fifth chapter of Galatians describes this working of the Spirit of God as the fruits of "love, joy, peace, patience, kindness, generosity, faithfulness, gentleness and self-control" (Gal 5:22, NRSV). . . . [These fruits] are dynamic sources of growth in us. These gifts of sacred life, alive and pulsing, move through our inner being like blood pumped from the heart through the whole system. . . . [They] move us toward action.

We can choose whether or not to act. . . . The poet Jessica Powers writes that the person who experiences the wind of the Spirit "turns like a wandering weather-vane toward love."[1] We always have the option to resist this turning. The choice is ours.

Endnote

1. Morneau, Robert, Siegfried, Regina, editors. *Selected Poetry of Jessica Powers*. Kansas City: Sheed and Ward, 1989, p. 38.

For Reflection

1. According to the reading from Acts of the Apostles as well as the selection from Rupp, what transformations took place in Jesus' followers gathered in the upper room on the day of Pentecost?

2. How does Rupp say she remains attentive to the workings of the Spirit in her own life?

3. Rupp reflects on the verb *poured* in Romans 5:5. Why does she find the word *poured* significant in relation to God's love for us?

4. Toward the end of the reading, Rupp lists the fruits of the Spirit. She says we can choose to act upon these energies. Describe someone you know or have heard of whose actions seem to embody one of these energies.

Part 5
Our New Life in Christ

17 Life in Heaven

Introduction

How do Christians respond to the death of a loved one? We may have been taught all our lives that Heaven is real; but when we lose someone, many of us have to journey through depression and doubt before we can fully embrace the hope for Heaven.

In this chapter's reading, James R. Kelly, a retired college professor whose wife died of breast cancer, traces the steps of his journey toward "a hope born of faith." Kelly, who had been raised in the rhythms of the traditional Catholic household, relied on prayer as he prepared for his wife's death during her long illness. Yet as this article reveals, he struggled to understand the concept of Heaven in light of his dwindling faith after Mary Lou's death.

Kelly describes how he and his wife settled into a comfortable pattern in the day-to-day functioning of their household during her final illness. Through prayer they learned to rely on God, listening for what God was asking of them each day. But when Mary Lou died, Kelly was surprised by his reaction. Not only was he overcome with grief, he says, but he also became desperate for answers to his questions about the afterlife; he wondered where Mary Lou is now. He sank into depression.

The end of the essay, and of Kelly's personal journey toward faith in the reality of Heaven, is touching. He discovered something that has enabled him to push away his questions and embrace the mystery of life after death, accepting that it truly is beyond our understanding. Kelly and his wife learned to trust in God's voice during her illness—now, years after Mary Lou's death, Kelly can help us see that trusting God's voice is also the key to faith in eternal life in Heaven.

"When Death Will Not Leave: A Husband's Journey Through Grief"

By James R. Kelly

My wife died at 5:30 a.m. on an October day more than eight years ago. At her wake, I told her many colleagues from the school where she had taught for over 30 years that the time of her death was fitting, because this was the time she would get up to get ready for school. And after all, dying can be easier than facing students.

For the Irish, making jokes is one of the things you think you should do at wakes, perhaps because laughing together is one of the more direct foreshadowings of heaven. But the line got no laughs. That too is okay, as a failed joke might be a direct foreshadowing of purgatory. The non-joke turned out to be an omen.

Mary Lou died before her time: before 60, before retirement, before Social Security, before our son finished college, before I told her everything I wanted to say. She died of breast cancer, so we couldn't think of ourselves as being singled out; we were part of a huge statistic (and with health insurance, a less unfortunate part of that statistic). Still, given her utterly responsible habits, she should have been among those many who, at least in the ads, are smilingly, confidently and glamorously not only still alive but—how American—racing for the cure. She always took the recommended yearly Pap test and mammogram. When her cancer was first diagnosed in mid-1990, her doctor congratulated herself on how well Mary Lou's mastectomy had gone. Still, Mary Lou did the maximum: radiation treatment, chemotherapy, drugs like Tamoxifen and Fosamax.

I thought we had left it behind us, and life went on as before: Mary Lou and I teaching, our son growing into adolescence, Grandpa visiting every Sunday, family events, the Mets losing. It was a shock that day in 1997 when Mary's oncologist told us the annual scan showed some cancer, just a trace, in the lung area. I believed his tone and his message just as I had the first time: "We're here early. Just some radiation and chemo and we'll be fine." But one day a year and a half later Mary awoke to find she couldn't raise her right arm. Twelve hours later in the emergency room, we learned that the cancer had spread to her brain.

Praying Apart and Together

More radiation could only stave off the inevitable, but it made it possible for her to attend our son's high school graduation. Home hospice care followed. During this time a friend asked whether we were planning a trip to Lourdes. This had never occurred to either of us. An attenuated sense of Mary's place in the Catholic understanding of the mystery of providence was not the reason for our inattention. After Sunday Mass at Our Lady of Angels, Mary Lou would always go to the statue of Our Lady to the left of the main altar and pray. Our son Jim and I would remain in the pew until she finished. From time to time I now go to the same spot and I say, "My prayer is whatever Mary Lou was praying." It wasn't that I doubted miracles might happen at Lourdes, but it seemed to me as likely to happen in Brooklyn as in France.

Mary Lou and I both prayed daily but not together, save for one succinct practice. I do not recall how it began—though it was when she was in Stage 4 cancer—but it was simple, and we did it right after breakfast and right before she would soon have to return wearily to bed. It was a couplet from Psalm 95, which often appeared as the response to the psalm on Sunday: "If today you hear his voice, harden not your heart." It appealed to us for two reasons. The reminder not to harden your heart was always timely, though more necessary for me than for her. But also, and this especially appealed to Mary, it felt right each day to remind ourselves that no matter what our feeble powers of body and mind and spirit, we must listen to what God is asking at that moment. Illnesses, even final ones, do not change the essentials. This snippet of psalm became so important to us that I had it placed on the memorial cards for the wake.

That wake was a long time coming. We fell into a rhythm that I thought would never end. Mary Lou wore a wig and could not eat whole foods; and Häagen-Dazs and Carvel ice cream, formerly weekend treats, were now her daily sustenance. I had a reduced teaching schedule with no departmental obligations, and the two days a week when I was not home, a longtime family friend would stay with her. She was there the morning Mary Lou died.

Implausibility of Faith

One would think that after many months death's arrival would be no surprise, but even expected deaths bring unexpected reactions. I was shocked by the onrush of cold grief and the abyss of loneliness that followed the blur of the wake, the funeral liturgy, the burial, the gathering back at the house and the task of responding to hundreds of condolences. I was most surprised by what happened to my faith. For a standard Catholic of my generation (and probably a standard Jew and a standard Muslim), faith is so thoroughly intermeshed with daily life—liturgies, Sunday family Mass, holidays, baptisms, prayers—that even the shock and long siege of cancer is not daunting. But when the **quotidian** itself is smashed, one's faith can change dramatically. My faith didn't go away, but it shrank, making the safely mysterious now seem wildly **implausible**—not unbelievable, but implausible. Details that had been part of a grand, sweeping and essentially joyous narrative suddenly required minute inspection, and things that were background suddenly become foreground. I started reading the catechism for things I thought I knew but no longer remembered as specifics. All of a sudden, the specifics mattered. Was Mary judged immediately and sent to heaven (or to purgatory)? What is the relationship between the cosmic last judgment and our particular judgment? If Catholics join their bodies in heaven only after the final judgment, does that mean no heaven—or at least no complete heaven—after the particular judgment? And (though its contribution to hell seemed more obvious) what would the addition of a body bring to heaven, since, as Jesus told the Sadducees, "at the resurrection men and women do not marry; they are like angels in heaven"?

A Note from the Past

Some dreary years later I found a note that Mary Lou had placed in my suitcase before I went off to an annual convention. It was always a trip involving some anxiety about a paper that I was to give; silly now, but a big deal then. The note was short and simple and commonsensical and magical: "Hi sweetheart! Relax! See you

quotidian Everyday, commonplace.
implausible Unlikely.

soon. Love, Mary." It soon became the focus of my daily prayer and the start of the end of my depression. Unlike the mental health drugs which cannot cure death and can bring only numbness, Mary's words, which sacramentally had now become a prayer, pushed to the very back of my consciousness all those specific theological implausibilities that arise from a faith unmoored from the anchor of the quotidian. What the catechism says about death now made perfect sense to me: that our afterlife is "beyond all understanding and description" and can only be captured by images, like "wedding feast" or "heavenly Jerusalem." Or now in a note, found years after a death, saying, "See you soon." It seemed inharmonious with the universe, a betrayal of creation, that Mary's words could not be true.

And so, I told myself, I should listen to her and relax. Try to teach. Try to be a friend. Go back to losing at tennis. Watch the Mets lose. Believe in her words: "See you soon." I realize that this is a faith born of hope and a hope born of faith rather than anything strictly evidentiary. But making Mary's note a prayer allows me to say once again, "If today you hear his voice, harden not your heart." Without a prayer like this, there could be no worthy life. Death makes a numbed heart inevitable;

> " *I realize that this is a faith born of hope and a hope born of faith.* "

but numbness must not let itself become a hardened heart, which may be the core definition of death. We are reminded in the catechism that "We cannot be united with God unless we freely choose to love him," with a citation of 1 Jn 3:14–15: "He who does not love remains in death."

A year after finding Mary's note I had the cemetery add to the family gravestone that line from Psalm 95: "If today you hear his voice, harden not your heart." In lieu of a miracle, I had found a sacramental sign.

For Reflection

1. What range of reactions to Mary Lou's death does Kelly describe, beginning with his behavior at the wake?

2. Why was the couplet from Psalm 95 significant to Kelly and his wife during her illness? Why do you think he put it on the family gravestone?

3. In your own words, explain how hope and faith are intertwined in Kelly's experience.

18 The Grace to Be Holy

Introduction

Holiness. Stop for a moment and let an image form in your imagination. What comes to mind when you think of holiness? Some might imagine a quiet church; others might picture a religious sister or priest. Some might see a figure from the Bible or a beloved saint. Still others might go a different direction and imagine a serene natural setting, like a night sky or a sun-dappled path in the woods.

The word *holiness* evokes unique personal associations for each of us, but you may be surprised to learn how the Church envisions holiness. One of the documents of Vatican Council II, *Dogmatic Constitution on the Church* (*Lumen Gentium*), contains a chapter titled "The Universal Call to Holiness in the Church." The first excerpt that follows comes from that chapter.

Let's look at the Council's phrase "universal call to holiness in the Church," because it highlights an important aspect of Church teaching on holiness. You probably know that the Church uses the term *vocation* to talk about God's plan for our lives. A vocation is a calling from God to fulfill a particular purpose or mission in life. Notice the term *universal call*.

Why Is It Called *Lumen Gentium*?

Like most official writings issued by the popes and the Vatican, the documents of Vatican Council II were written in Latin and then translated into many languages. On the Vatican Web site, you can find twelve translations of this document. "*Lumen gentium*" is not strictly the title; rather, it is the opening phrase of the original Latin text. This translates to "the Light of nations" in English, or "*nemzetek világossága*" in Hungarian.

In this case *universal* means that the call to holiness goes out to all people. *Dogmatic Constitution on the Church* emphasizes that no matter what our life situation is, we all are called to be holy.

This excerpt from the Council offers many glimpses of what holiness may involve, and you will see the word *charity* more than once. Charity, a gift that God gives us, is a unique kind of love. By means of charity, we love God above all things, and out of that love of God, we love our neighbors as ourselves. In this excerpt you will find many ways God helps us to fulfill the

"J. P. Two, We Love You!"

Karol Wojtyła was elected Pope in 1978, serving as the beloved "Polish Pope" John Paul II until his death in 2005. As Archbishop of Krakow, he was among the Church leaders who drafted the statements of Vatican Council II. Saint John Paul II traveled more widely than any previous Pope, and he was the first to travel in the popemobile. He instituted the first World Youth Day in 1985, bringing together young people from around the world, who often chanted, "J. P. Two, we love you!" He was beatified in 2010 and canonized in 2014.

call to holiness. The Council also reminds us that in order to grow in holiness, we must pray and make every effort to become more and more like Christ in our own lives.

The second excerpt in this chapter is from *Crossing the Threshold of Hope*, by Saint John Paul II, the Pope your parents' generation learned about as teenagers. This reading offers encouragement in the struggle to fulfill our calling to holiness, or our vocation, from God. The message of hope in this short reading is that God will help us to respond to his call. "The Gospel is certainly demanding," Saint John Paul II acknowledges (p. 222), and we should not fool ourselves into thinking otherwise. But we can take strength from knowing that God always offers us the grace to meet those demands.

Excerpt from *Dogmatic Constitution on the Church* (*Lumen Gentium*)

By the Second Vatican Council

40. The Lord Jesus, the divine Teacher and Model of all perfection, preached holiness of life to each and every one of His disciples of every condition. He Himself stands as the author and consummator of this holiness of life: "Be you therefore perfect, even as your heavenly Father is perfect" (Mt. 5:48).[1] Indeed He sent the Holy Spirit upon all men that He might move them inwardly to love God with their whole heart and their whole soul, with all their mind and all their strength (cf. Mk. 12:30) and that they might love each other as Christ loves them (cf. Jn. 13.34; 15:12). The followers of Christ are called by God, not because of their works, but according to His own purpose and grace. They are **justified** in the Lord Jesus, because in the baptism of faith they truly become sons of God and sharers in the divine nature. In this way they are really made holy. Then too, by God's gift, they must hold on to and complete in their lives this holiness they have received. They are warned by the Apostle to live "as becomes saints" (Eph. 5:3), and to put on "as God's chosen ones, holy and beloved a heart of mercy, kindness, humility, meekness, patience" (Col. 3:12), and to possess the fruit of the Spirit in holiness (cf. Gal. 5:22; Rom. 6:22). Since truly we all offend in many things (cf. Jas. 3:2) we all need God's mercies continually and we all must daily pray: "Forgive us our debts" (Mt. 6:12).[2] Thus it is evident to everyone, that all the faithful of Christ of whatever rank or status, are called to the fullness of the Christian life and to the perfection of charity;[3] by this holiness as such a more human manner of living is promoted in this earthly society. In order that the faithful may reach this perfection, they must use their strength accordingly as they have received it, as a gift from Christ. They must follow in His footsteps and conform themselves to His image seeking the will of the Father in all things. They must devote themselves with all their being to the glory

justified Freed by God from the guilt of sin.

of God and the service of their neighbor. In this way, the holiness of the People of God will grow into an abundant harvest of good, as is admirably shown by the life of so many saints in Church history.

41. The classes and duties of life are many, but holiness is one—that sanctity which is cultivated by all who are moved by the Spirit of God, and who obey the voice of the Father and worship God the Father in spirit and in truth. These people follow the poor Christ, the humble and cross-bearing Christ in order to be worthy of being sharers in His glory. Every person must walk unhesitatingly according to his own personal gifts and duties in the path of living faith, which arouses hope and works through charity.

Endnotes

1. Cfr. S. Gregorius M., Hom in Evang. 19, 1: PL 76, 1154 B. S Augustinus, Serm. 341, 9, 11: PL 39, 1499 s. S. Io. Damascenus, Adv. Iconocl. 11: PG 96, 1357.
2. Cfr. S. Irenaeus, adv. Haer, 111 24, 1: PG 7, 966 B; Harvey 2, 13i, ed. Sagnard, Sources Chr., p 398.
3. S. Cyprianus, De Orat Dom. 23: PL 4, 5S3, Hartel, III A, p. 28S. S. Augustinus, Serm. 71, 20, 33: PL 38, 463 s. S. Io. Damascenus, Adv. Iconocl. 12: PG 96, 1358 D.

Excerpt from *Crossing the Threshold of Hope*

By Pope Saint John Paul II

When, on October 22, 1978, I said the words "Be not afraid!" in St. Peter's Square, I could not fully know how far they would take me and the entire Church. Their meaning came more from the Holy Spirit, the Consoler promised by the Lord Jesus to His disciples, than from the man who spoke them. Nevertheless, with the passing of the years, I have recalled these words on many occasions.

The exhortation "Be not afraid!" should be interpreted as having a very broad meaning. In a certain sense *it was an exhortation addressed to all people,* an exhortation to conquer fear in the present world situation, as much in the East as in the West, as much in the North as in the South.

Have no fear of that which you yourselves have created, have no fear of all that man has produced, and that every day is becoming more dangerous for him! Finally, have no fear of yourselves!

Why should we have no fear? Because man has been redeemed by God. When pronouncing these words in St. Peter's Square, I already knew that my first encyclical and my entire papacy would be tied to the truth of the Redemption. In the Redemption we find the most profound basis for the words "Be not afraid!": "For God so loved the world that he gave his only Son" (cf. Jn 3:16). This Son is always present in the history of humanity as Redeemer. The Redemption pervades all of human history, even before Christ, and prepares its eschatological future. It is the light that "shines in the darkness, and the darkness has not overcome it" (cf. Jn 1:5). *The power of Christ's Cross and Resurrection is greater than any evil which man could or should fear.* . . .

. . . Peoples and nations of the entire world need to hear these words. *Their conscience needs to grow in the certainty that Someone exists who holds in His hands the destiny of this passing world; Someone who holds the keys to death and the netherworld* (cf. Rev 1:18); *Someone who is* **the Alpha and the Omega** *of human history* (cf. Rev 22:13)—be it the individual or collective history. And this Someone is Love (cf. 1 Jn 4:8, 16)—Love that became man, Love crucified and risen, Love unceasingly present among men. It is Eucharistic Love. It is the infinite source of communion. He alone can give the ultimate assurance when He says "Be not afraid!"

You observe that contemporary man finds it hard to return to faith because he is afraid of the moral demands that faith makes upon him. And this, to a certain degree, is the truth. *The Gospel is certainly demanding.* We know that Christ never permitted His disciples and those who listened to Him to entertain any illusions about this. On the contrary, He spared no effort in preparing them for every type of internal or external difficulty, always aware of the fact that they might well decide to abandon Him. Therefore, if He says, "Be not afraid!" He certainly does not say it in order to **nullify** in some way that which He has required. Rather, by these words He confirms the entire truth of

the Alpha and the Omega The first and last letters of the Greek alphabet, used to mean the "be-all and end-all."

nullify To invalidate, or make something ineffective.

the Gospel and all the demands it contains. At the same time, however, He reveals that *His demands never exceed man's abilities*. If man accepts these demands with an attitude of faith, he will also find in the grace that God never fails to give him the necessary strength to meet those demands. The world

> *It is very important to cross the threshold of hope,* not to stop before it, but *to let oneself be led.*

is full of proof of the saving and redemptive power that the Gospels proclaim with even greater frequency than they recall demands of the moral life. How many people there are in the world whose daily lives attest to the possibility of living out the morality of the Gospel! Experience shows that a successful human life cannot be other than a life like theirs.

To accept the Gospel's demands means to affirm all of our humanity, to see in it the beauty desired by God, while at the same time recognizing, in light of the power of God Himself, our weaknesses: "What is impossible for men is possible for God" (Lk 18:27).

These two dimensions cannot be separated: on the one hand, the moral demands God makes of man; on the other, the demands of His saving love—the gift of His grace—to which God in a certain sense has bound Himself. What else is the Redemption accomplished in Christ, if not precisely this? *God desires the salvation of man, He desires that humanity find that fulfillment to which He Himself has destined it,* and Christ has the right to say that His yoke is easy and His burden, in the end, light (cf. Mt 11:30).

It is very important to cross the threshold of hope, not to stop before it, but *to let oneself be led.*

For Reflection

1. In the first excerpt, Vatican Council II emphasizes that all believers are called to a life of holiness. What descriptions of holiness do you find in the excerpt?

2. The Council states that our collective holiness will "grow into an abundant harvest of good." Give examples of that "harvest of good."

3. In the second excerpt, Pope Saint John Paul II writes that Redemption is the basis for the words "Be not afraid." Explain this idea in your own words.

4. The Pope suggests that people find it hard to be faithful because they are afraid of the moral demands of faith. Give examples of moral demands young people today may fear. What advice do you imagine Saint John Paul II would offer you, based on this reading?

19 Accepting Jesus' Teaching

Introduction

Imagine a living room in England during World War II. It is 2:45 on a Sunday afternoon in November; the year is 1942. The family gathers around a large radio for an interesting program that has been airing at 2:50 for the last few Sundays. Everyone settles into chairs with cups of tea, now precious due to wartime rationing. They are preparing to listen to the latest installment of *Christian Behaviour* with C. S. Lewis.

The reading in this chapter is from a book by the same name, a collection of the eight talks Lewis delivered in 1942 on **BBC** radio. Lewis was a scholar of English literature who himself wrote many types of literature. By 1942 his published works already included poetry, science fiction, scholarly studies, and popular theology. He also presented more than twenty radio talks on Christianity. Lewis, a member of the Church of England, is regarded by some as one of the most influential Christian writers of the twentieth century.

In one of his radio talks, Lewis explored two meanings of faith: (1) belief in

Narnia and Middle Earth

C. S. Lewis is perhaps best known as the author of the Chronicles of Narnia. You may be surprised to learn that Lewis rejected his Christian upbringing before he was fifteen. Nearly twenty years passed before he could again say he believed in God; but even then he was not ready to return to the Church of England until a fellow writer, a devout Catholic, convinced him that Jesus Christ was the Son of God. That writer? J. R. R. Tolkien, author of *The Lord of the Rings.*

BBC British Broadcasting Company.

the truth of the doctrines of Christianity, and (2) trust in God's eternal goodness. The excerpt you will read here, drawn from that radio talk, focuses on the first meaning. Lewis considers why the Church regards the belief in Christian teachings to be a virtue. He traces his own thought process for his audience, explaining that reason alone does not control our belief in a doctrine, or even in an observable fact. Our moods, our imagination, and our emotions, he explains, may attack our beliefs, eroding and ultimately destroying them. He concludes that to stand firm in our beliefs about the revealed truth, we must train "the habit of Faith" to defend ourselves against the onslaught of irrational influences. The excerpt includes several suggestions for strengthening our beliefs.

Notice the method that Lewis uses to convince the radio audience of the truth of his positions. Moving step-by-step through his argument, providing concrete examples to illustrate his thinking, he leads his listener to the logical conclusion. Much of Lewis's writing, along with his radio addresses, fall into the literary category of Christian apology—that is, writings that aim to convince the reader of the truth of Christianity.

Of course, Lewis recognizes that faith is far more than believing the truths of Christianity; those beliefs are the foundation for the deeper meaning of faith, faith as complete trust in God. But understanding this first meaning of faith—the virtue of belief itself—reminds us to nurture our own belief, just as we would nurture any other virtue. Belief is not something we either have or do not have, any more than kindness is. Those who are kind have worked hard to cultivate that virtue. How will we cultivate faith?

Excerpt from *Christian Behaviour*
By C. S. Lewis

Faith

Roughly speaking, the word Faith seems to be used by Christians in two senses or on two levels, and I will take them in turn. In the first sense it means simply Belief—accepting or regarding as true the doctrines of Christianity. That is fairly simple. But what does puzzle people—at least it used to puzzle me—is the fact that Christians regard faith in this sense as a virtue. I used to ask how on earth it can be a virtue—what is there moral or immoral about believing or not believing a set of statements? Obviously, I used to say, a sane man accepts or rejects any statement, not because he wants or does not want to, but because the evidence seems to him good or bad. If he were mistaken about the goodness or badness of the evidence that would not mean he was a bad man, but only that he was not very clever. And if he thought the evidence bad but tried to force himself to believe in spite of it, that would be merely stupid.

Well, I think I still take that view. But what I did not see then—and a good many people do not see still—was this. I was assuming that if the human mind once accepts a thing as true it will automatically go on regarding it as true, until some real reason for reconsidering it turns up. In fact, I was assuming that the human mind is completely ruled by reason. But that is not so. For example, my reason is perfectly convinced by good evidence that anaesthetics do not smother me and that properly trained surgeons do not start operating until I am unconscious. But the idea does not alter the fact that when they have me down on the table and clap their horrible mask over my face, a mere childish panic begins inside me. I start thinking I am going to choke, and I am afraid they will start cutting me up before I am properly under. In other words, I lose my faith in anaesthetics. It is not reason that is taking away my faith: on the contrary, my faith is based on reason. It is my imagination and emotions. The battle is between faith and reason on one side and emotion and imagination on the other.

When you think of it you will see lots of instances of this. A man knows, on perfectly good evidence, that a . . . [woman] of his acquaintance is a liar and cannot keep a secret and ought not to be trusted; but when he finds himself with her his mind loses its faith in that bit of knowledge and he starts thinking, "Perhaps she'll be different this time," and once more makes a fool of himself and tells her something he ought not to have told her. His senses and emotions have destroyed his faith in what he really knows to be true. Or take a boy learning to swim. His reason knows perfectly well that an unsupported human body will not necessarily sink in water: he has seen dozens of people float and swim.

But the whole question is whether he will be able to go on believing this when the instructor takes away his hand and leaves him unsupported in the water—or whether he will suddenly cease to believe it and get in a fright and go down.

> 66 *Faith . . . is the art of holding on to things your reason has once accepted, in spite of your changing moods.* 99

Now just the same thing happens about Christianity. I am not asking anyone to accept Christianity if his best reasoning tells him that the weight of the evidence is against it. That is not the point at which Faith comes in. But supposing a man's reason once decides that the weight of the evidence is for it. I can tell that man what is going to happen to him in the next few weeks. There will come a moment when there is bad news, or he is in trouble, or is living among a lot of other people who do not believe it, and all at once his emotions will rise up and carry out a sort of **blitz** on his belief. Or else there will come a moment when he . . . wants to tell a lie, or feels very pleased with himself, or sees a chance of making a little money in some way that is not perfectly fair: some moment, in fact, at which it would be very convenient if Christianity were not true. And once again his wishes and desires will carry out a blitz. I am not talking of moments at which any real new reasons against Christianity turn up. Those have to be faced and that is a different matter. I am talking about moments where a mere mood rises up against it.

Now Faith, in the sense in which I am here using the word, is the art of holding on to things your reason has once accepted, in spite of your changing moods. For moods will change, whatever view your reason takes.

I know that by experience. Now that I am a Christian I do have moods in which the whole thing looks very improbable: but when I was an atheist I had moods in

blitz An intense, sudden attack; short for *blitzkrieg*. Lewis's radio listeners likely associated the word with the Blitz—Germany's air assaults on Britain in World War II.

which Christianity looked terribly probable. This rebellion of your moods against your real self is going to come anyway. That is why Faith is such a necessary virtue: unless you teach your moods "where they get off," you can never be either a sound Christian or even a sound atheist, but just a creature dithering to and fro, with its beliefs really dependent on the weather and the state of its digestion. Consequently one must train the habit of Faith.

The first step is to recognise the fact that your moods change. The next is to make sure that, if you have once accepted Christianity, then some of its main doctrines shall be deliberately held before your mind for some time every day. That is why daily prayers and religious reading and church-going are necessary parts of the Christian life. We have to be continually reminded of what we believe. Neither this belief nor any other will automatically remain alive in the mind. It must be fed. And as a matter of fact, if you examined a hundred people who had lost their faith in Christianity, I wonder how many of them would turn out to have been reasoned out of it by honest argument? Do not most people simply drift away?

For Reflection

1. According to Lewis, what causes a person to judge whether something is true?

2. Lewis provides several examples to show that more than reason influences our minds. Name some influences today that may attack your mind's ability to believe Jesus' teachings.

3. Lewis explains why accepting the truth of Christian teachings is a virtue. Explain his reasoning in your own words.

4. What strategies does Lewis suggest for strengthening our belief in the truths of Christianity?

20 A Sacramental Life

Introduction

Have you ever grabbed your phone or laptop as you were about to leave the house, only to realize that you forgot to charge it? We rely on our electronic devices, but they are not much good without a regular connection to a power source.

In the first reading in this chapter, Dr. Jerry Shepherd, a teacher and former headmaster at a Catholic high school, describes the Sacraments of the Church as a "readily available power source" (p. 31)—not for our phones and laptops, but rather for us. That is because each Sacrament is a source of God's grace. Shepherd explains how the Sacraments offer us the graces, the power, we need as we move through our lives. Each Sacrament, he says, corresponds to a time in our lives when God's gracious help enables us to fulfill his Divine Will. Shepherd emphasizes that the Sacraments do not just offer us a sense of comfort or support; they actually strengthen us to do God's will.

Greek Orthodox catechist and religious education director Anna Nicole Kyritsis agrees that the Sacraments are necessary for the Christian life. In the second reading, she examines the metaphor of a silversmith (from Malachi 3:3) to explain how the Sacraments purify us so that the image of Christ in us can shine forth in all that we are and do. But Kyritsis also urges us to engage in sacramental living. She says we must do more than receive the Sacraments in Church: sacramental living "entails living every moment in the footsteps of Christ" (p. 29).

Greek Orthodox One of the churches within the communion of Eastern Orthodox Churches that developed in the Eastern Roman Empire and that does not recognize the authority of the Pope.

Throughout the reading Kyritsis stresses that the Sacraments are central to the Christian life—she is not arguing that we do not need the Sacraments. When we share in the Sacraments, we become united to Christ. Her point, however, is that the Sacraments are not the only way for us to draw nearer to Christ. We also become united with him through prayerfully studying God's Word and putting Jesus' teachings into practice.

> **Christ's Light in Us**
>
> Have you ever left Mass or even confession only to catch yourself just a short while later behaving in a way that contradicts Gospel values? To live as followers of Christ and truly reflect the grace we receive in the Sacraments, we must allow Christ's light to shine in us by striving to make God's will the center of our lives.

Both selections in this chapter use the term *real* to describe an aspect of our life with God. Shepherd opens by saying, "Real life must come from Christ" (p. 31). When we unite ourselves to Christ, allowing him to live in us, our lives have real value. We share in the life of Christ through the Sacraments. Kyritsis also uses the adjective *real* and concludes by reminding us to make Christ real within ourselves by living a sacramental life. These two ways of experiencing Christ's life bracket the readings: We share in Christ's life when we take part in the Sacraments, and we allow that life to shine forth when we live as he did.

Excerpt from *Teens and Spirituality*
By Jerry Shepherd

Real Life

Real life must come from Christ. "I came that they may have life, and have it abundantly" (John 10:10).

> " *For our lives to have real value, we must live Christ's life.* "

For our lives to have real value, we must live Christ's life. He gives us that life in grace, especially and most surely through the sacraments he has entrusted to the Church. On earth, they are our never-ending, readily available power source, our energizers in the spiritual life.

The sacraments parallel our own sense of the particular stages of ordinary life. We remain dead until we are born to the life of grace through Baptism. We need food to keep living, so Christ gives us himself. He becomes literally "our daily bread" that we may grow every day more like him. We begin to enter more fully into deep, personal relationships with others. Confirmation is the sacrament that leads us to a more intimate union with Christ and creates in us a stronger sense of belonging to the Church. For most of us, marriage is the grand decision of our lives, one that will shape and condition our future for as long as our spouse lives, and a decision that involves new demands and concerns. Thus, we are grateful that marriage is a sacrament, blessed by Christ himself, and full of graces that will help us in our new state. The same is true of Holy Orders, should the priesthood be God's way for us. Then throughout life we are aware that we can use our freedom to reject God's gifts. To answer this weakness, Christ provides the sacrament of Penance. And when we face illness or even death, with its pressure for an ultimate choice and its apparent finality, we surely feel the need for the succor of the Anointing of the Sick.

The groupings of the sacraments in the *Catechism of the Catholic Church* also suggest our need for them. The sacraments of Christian initiation—Baptism, Confirmation, and the Eucharist—respond to our need to have the spiritual life in us begun, deepened, and fed. The sacraments of healing—Penance and the Anointing of the Sick—speak to our continuing weakness in mind, body, and will, and to our need to be forgiven. The sacraments of service—Matrimony and Holy Orders—fulfill our need to love and be loved and to give ourselves to others as Christ gave himself to us.

In other words, whenever the ordinary person in an ordinary life sees and feels the need of special help, the sacraments, with their particular graces, are there to provide it. If they only gave psychological comfort, they would still be wonderful enough for most of us weak creatures. But, in fact, each actually increases our power to do what God wills and to be happy doing it at the major crossroads of our lives . . . if only we will use them.

Excerpt from "Living the Sacramental Life"
By Anna Nicole Kyritsis

One year at a Lenten youth retreat, three teenagers attended an Orthodox Life session entitled, "Living a Sacramental Life." The facilitator's goal was to reveal that our Lord instructs us to live the Sacraments, rather than simply to partake of them. He illustrated his point through several scriptural references, both from the Old Testament and the New Testament, that revealed God's instructions for living. . . . These three young adults became baffled by one of the speaker's examples, a quote taken from Malachi. "He will sit as a refiner and purifier of silver" (Malachi 3:3). Although they could not comprehend how that particular scripture related to God's instructions to live the sacramental life, upon departing the retreat, the three decided to research further and discovered how this example correlated to the lesson.

During the next week one of the trio made an appointment to visit and watch a silversmith at work. She watched him heat a piece of silver by holding it over the fire. During this process he explained to her that the silver needs to be placed in the center of the fire, where the flames are the hottest in order to burn away all of the metal's impurities. Furthermore, he showed her that he had to keep his eyes on the piece of silver the entire time it was immersed in the fire, so as to prevent it from spoiling. For, if the silver remains in the flames for too long, then it will be destroyed. The young lady was intrigued as to how the silversmith timed the heating process. "How do you know when the silver is fully refined?" Smiling at her, he responded, "Oh, that's simple. The silver is refined and purified when I see my image in it."

. . . Just as the silversmith reveals that the silver must be cleansed of its impurities so that he may see in it his image, so must we be cleansed of our impurities in order to mirror the likeness of Christ. Although our sins are forgiven through repentance and the sacraments of Confession and

Communion, we still have the capacity to sin again. Jesus Christ designed a way of life for His disciples to follow in order to live a life created in His likeness. Within this plan, Christ instituted a series of visible sacraments to promote the communion of one's life with His. The Holy Sacraments are a means that allow us to repent, to be forgiven, to receive both physical and spiritual healing and strengthening, and to be saved. We all know this, right? . . . Think again. Sacramental living is more than being baptized and putting on Christ as a child. It requires more commitment than receiving Holy Communion on Sunday. It demands more than confessing one's sins once a year. It entails living every moment in the footsteps of Christ so that we may be prepared to receive His glorious Kingdom.

. . . Sacramental living is also a continual process. Each breath that we take enables us to enjoy another moment of the life that God gave to each of us. Within every moment that we live, we should walk in the footsteps of Christ. The Holy Sacraments aid us in this process by making God real to us through the five senses. However, because they are not always available to us at every moment of the day, we need to do more.

So how should we live a sacramental life? Simple. We should invite Christ into our life. One should make Him the center of one's daily routine. Christ teaches that through prayer we may receive help and understanding of His will for us. He shows us upon His death that, above all else, we should love and forgive our enemies as well as our neighbors. He beseeches us to deny ourselves and follow Him. Within each of these practices lay deeds and actions that will bring us closer to living a sacramental life. . . .

Just as the silversmith immersed the piece of silver in the fire to cleanse it from its impurities, so must we immerse ourselves . . . in Christ to purify our souls. Yet, the full immersion does not end with the participation in the Holy Sacraments, but requires us to study Christ's living example and the lives of the saints, to read and study the Holy Bible, to engage in a consistent prayer life, to live according to Christ's teachings, commandments, and God's will, and to witness to others . . . through our own living examples. For Christ, too, desires to see His image in us, which necessitates that we lead sacramental lives. However, living such lives requires us to go beyond the set Sacraments so that we may receive God's grace. Therefore, we must commit to making Him real within ourselves on a daily basis.

For Reflection

1. Shepherd's reading begins with a quotation from the Gospel of John about abundant life. Looking at his explanation of the graces offered in the Sacraments, how do you think this author would describe abundant life?

2. Shepherd says that the Sacraments will help us do God's will happily. Why do you think Shepherd adds, "if only we will use them"?

3. In the second reading, Kyritsis describes how a silversmith purifies silver. Explain this metaphor in your own words. What are some things the silversmith does that God also does?

4. Kyritsis describes how the silversmith immerses the silver in fire to purify it. What are her suggestions for immersing ourselves in Christ, who will purify our souls? Which of her suggestions comes most easily to you? Which do you find most difficult?

Part 6
Prayer and Our Life in Christ

21 Why We Pray

Introduction

Why pray? This is a good question, and it is the title of the first chapter in *Challenges in Prayer,* by M. Basil Pennington. And he should know: Pennington was a Trappist monk for more than fifty years. Trappists, members of the Cistercian Order of the Strict Observance, are contemplative monks, dedicated to a life of work and prayer. The monks follow Saint Benedict's sixth-century **rule** for monasteries: They live a simple life of silence and solitude, spending much of their day in prayer.

Before his death in 2005, Pennington published fifty-seven books and many more articles. He traveled widely, visiting, advising, and learning from other monks worldwide. In his writing and lectures, he taught about centering prayer and *lectio divina,* a form of meditation that is often used as a contemplative way to read Scripture. By the end of his life, Pennington was respected around the world as a great spiritual master.

The Life of a Trappist Monk

At Saint Joseph's Abbey, a cloistered religious community in Spencer, Massachusetts, the monks rise at 3:10 a.m. By bedtime, at 8:00 p.m., they have gathered for communal prayer eight times and have taken time for personal prayer three times. They have also put in a five-hour work day. For much of the day, they have observed silence. As the monastery's Web site says, "The life of an enclosed monk is meant for relatively few."

rule A type of constitution that clarifies the mission and directs the daily life of a religious community or institute according to the spirit of the Gospel. Saint Benedict wrote one such rule, still used today by many religious orders.

In the selection in this chapter, Pennington shares his own reasons for praying. He starts with a description of how God works in our world and in our lives: God is a constant and ongoing presence. Moreover, Pennington explains how our very lives are completely immersed in the life of God. When we are baptized into Christ, we become one with him and share in his life.

Pennington describes the prayers arising from a heightened emotional state. He writes eloquently about how the beauty of nature fills his heart with praise and thanks. Suffering moves him to cry out to God for help. Many of us share these kinds of prayer experiences. They are spontaneous acts of faith, based on our belief that God is ultimately in charge and that he cares deeply about each of us.

This simple faith that God is in charge is something we can nurture. Pennington's daily life in the monastery—punctuated by communal prayer and structured to allow spiritual reading and quiet reflection—ensured that he would turn to God whenever his feelings took over. The Gifts of the Holy Spirit also helped him—and can help us—to be aware of God's presence, most especially the gifts of knowledge and understanding.

But prayer goes beyond reaching out to God in moments when we experience bursts of emotion. For Pennington, prayer is related to a theme found in many readings in this book: We are created in the image of God. Prayer is an act not only of faith but also of love. We are created in the image of the God who is Love. We also have a deep-seated need to be loved; and whether we are celibate monks, married people with a houseful of children, or teenagers with many friends and beloved family members, we are always looking for that most fulfilling, most trustworthy love that only God can offer us. If, like Pennington, we have built a relationship with God, uniting ourselves to him with the help of the Holy Spirit, we will find ourselves reaching out to God in prayer simply because we love him.

Excerpt from *Challenges in Prayer*

By M. Basil Pennington

This is why we should pray. Divine goodness and love postulate it. Divine goodness expressed in our being calls for it. We cannot be true to who we are, we cannot be integral, if we do not pray, and pray without ceasing.

But why do *I* pray?

I do try to ground my life on these fundamental facts. I try to make space in my life to get in touch with them through reading and meditation, to let them surface and influence my way of living and my response to life. But in fact, more often than not, it is the feeling, the emotion of the moment, that impels my prayer. True, if there were not deep-seated convictions forming my basic attitude to life and all reality, my response to these emotions would not be prayer. There might be some native mysticism. There would be a lot of despair. But hardly true prayer.

But, because my life is grounded on these convictions, when I am touched by a beautiful spring day—such as today—my heart does sing to our Creator. Spring is here and all creation seems to be springing forth. The brown fields take on a hopeful green. The sunsets and sunrises stop me short—pinks and reds and golds, clouds so close they can be felt, gently inviting Marian blues. Nature caresses, impresses. Buds burst from dried and gnarled vines and branches. There is hope for us all. Tulips and daffodils shoot up too quickly to be believed and splotch their bright colors on the recently dark canvas. Birds sing. Spring is here. God is here. My heart sings—sings to him as I go about the daily task or wander down forest trails or sit at my window and write this. It was in the midst of sweaty toil, clearing the marshes of **Clairvaux**, that Saint Bernard was inspired to write:

> I have experienced it, believe me! You find God more in the forests than in the books. Woods and stones will tell you things you cannot hear from teachers.

But it is not only spring that makes me sing. Each season—and I am prejudiced enough to say, especially in New England, though I am sure it is true elsewhere; I have found it everywhere I have gone—has its beauty and its call as it speaks to us of the beauty, the love, and the care of the Creator. And our only response can be prayer—prayer of praise, of thanksgiving, of love to love.

Isaiah 11:2 spoke of our Lord:

> The spirit of the LORD shall rest on him,
> the spirit of wisdom and understanding,
> the spirit of counsel and might,
> the spirit of knowledge and the fear of the LORD.

Patristic tradition came to speak of these as the Gifts of the Holy Spirit, seven dispositions formed in our spirit at baptism and activated by the Holy Spirit, when and how and to the degree he wishes, though certainly in response to our longings and aspirations. It is by the gifts of knowledge and understanding and the action of the Holy Spirit that we readily perceive the presence of the Creator in his creation, that we understand—"stand under" and see what lies beneath the surface (the Latin word for understand is *intelligere*—literally, to read within). When the gift of wisdom is activated, we even "taste and see that the Lord is sweet" (the Latin word for wisdom—*sapientia*—comes from *sapor*—savor). It is the activity of these precious gifts—our desire for this activity and our openness to it—that transforms not only glorious spring days, but every day and every experience, into constant prayer.

It is not only beauty and presence that calls forth prayer from my heart. It is also pain and hurt and apparent absence. These are the dark days, and they can come even when the sun is shining and the birds are singing. The cloud that obscures all this may be a cloud indeed: sin or the struggle with temptation, real tragedy—personal or communal—or physical pain. Or it may be objectively some real trivia (which I will realize when the sun finally does break through) that wounds my pride, thwarts my will, frustrates the hope of the moment. It may be a tempest in a teapot, but for the moment all is dark and stormy and I am very

Clairvaux The location of the first Cistercian monastery, in France. The monks had to clear marshland to build it.

threatened. I cry out, "Lord, save me, for I perish!" Why do I pray at such times? Because something deep within me repeats Peter's words: "Lord,

> *Being made in the likeness of God, we have been given hearts that have an infinite capacity for love.*

to whom shall we go? You have the words of eternal life" (John 6:68). In my anguish, and sometimes it is indeed bitter anguish (I am sure you know what I mean, having felt it, too), I need help, love, presence, and even though it may be very dark and lonely, the Spirit yet speaks to my spirit in words beyond my hearing. In some deep way I know there is hope, there is reason to cry out. There is One there beyond the clouds who hears.

But I pray not only when the sun is shining or the clouds are pressing and depressing. I pray all the time, because I need to pray all the time. *Caritas Christi urget nos*—The love of Christ compels us. We are loved with an **insatiable** love and our own love is insatiable.

God is love, and we are made to the image of God. It is of our very nature to love. And to love without limit. For, being made in the likeness of God, we have been given hearts that have an infinite capacity for love. Nothing less than a deep intense complete love affair with God—total communion (and what else is prayer in its fullness?)—will satisfy us, fulfill us. . . .

I could go on and on writing about this "why" of prayer. My whole life and yours is a "why" for prayer. The whole creation is, precisely because it is creation, a message of totally gratuitous love, love for us, to us. But do I really need to write anything at all? Let us just be still and *know* that he is God.

insatiable Incapable of being satisfied.

For Reflection

1. Pennington's love of nature is one basis for his prayer of praise and thanksgiving. Based on this reading, what other richly emotional experiences might prompt this type of prayer?

2. The author suggests that without a religious outlook on life, his response to his emotions would not be prayer. Why not? How can you, as a young person, promote this outlook for yourself?

3. Pennington says that his love for Christ "compels" him to pray: "I pray all the time, because I need to pray all the time." What do you think he means? Why does his love for Christ urge him to pray?

22 Learning to Pray

Introduction

Did you learn to pray when you were small? Do you remember your earliest lessons in prayer? Perhaps a parent or grandparent looked on while you recited simple bedtime prayers; maybe a parish catechist taught you the Lord's Prayer. You may have learned other prayers in school. But have you actually learned how to pray?

The reading in this chapter comes from *The Gift of Peace*, a memoir by Chicago's former archbishop Joseph Cardinal Bernardin. He begins, "I entered the seminary when I was only seventeen years old, and ever since then I have been trying to learn how to pray" (p. 4). When Bernardin wrote this memoir, he was in his sixties, a **cardinal** in the Church and a former president of the National Conference of Catholic Bishops. Yet he says he has long been "trying to learn how to pray." Evidently prayer is more than reciting words or learning methods. In this excerpt Bernardin writes honestly about his struggles over the years to "open the door of [his] soul" to God (p. 6).

In his book he reflects on the final years of his ministry. In a letter to the reader that begins *The Gift of Peace*, Bernardin describes the period the book covers by paraphrasing Charles Dickens: "It has been the best of times, it has been the worst of times" (p. ix). First, Bernardin faced a false accusation of sexual misconduct. In 1993, when the accusa-

cardinal A Church official appointed by the Pope to join the College of Cardinals, which advises the Pope. When a pope dies, that group elects one of its own members to be the next pope. Many cardinals are also bishops of dioceses.

tions aired on the national news, Bernardin was possibly the best-known and most widely respected leader in the U.S. Church. The former seminarian who brought the charges later admitted that the cardinal had not assaulted him. Bernardin sought out this young man and extended understanding and forgiveness. That experience filled Bernardin with new life, he writes; but shortly after that event, he was diagnosed with cancer. Determined to see himself as a priest first and a patient second, he often followed his radiation treatments with up to five hours of visiting other cancer patients.

As his illness progressed, he decided to write *The Gift of Peace*. Bernardin wanted to "help others understand how the good and the bad are always present in our human condition and, that if we 'let go,' if we place ourselves totally in the hands of the Lord, the good will prevail" (p. x).

To explain his journey through those years, Bernardin traces the development of his prayer life. He learned the importance of prayer as a teenager during seminary, he says, but as a busy priest committed to good works, he put prayer on the back burner. The Gospel demands that we serve our brothers and sisters, and the call to service was at the heart of Bernardin's life as a priest, bishop, and later cardinal. Yet service without a foundation in prayer is not Christian service. It is only in prayer that we truly come to know God's will—for ourselves and for those we serve.

Bernardin, who died from his illness in 1996, says here that his constant prayer was to be able to let go of everything that keeps him from surrendering to God's will. He clearly

Reconciliation and Return

After the case against Bernardin was dropped, he reached out to Steven Cook, the man who had falsely accused him of sexual misconduct. Cook, now very ill with HIV-AIDS, was eager to apologize to the cardinal. Cook had been abused by a different priest while studying at the seminary and had left the Church in anger. After accepting Bernardin's gift of an inscribed Bible, Cook agreed to the cardinal's invitation to celebrate Mass together.

reflected long and hard on his own resistance to God, exploring his inability to trust God fully. And that is the point: Prayer is about giving ourselves over to God. It means listening without distractions to God's will for our lives, and it means honestly sharing with God our fears and our needs. Prayer may begin with childhood bedtime prayers and later involve finding what works best for us, but prayer is really about opening our hearts and our lives to God.

Excerpt from *The Gift of Peace*
By Joseph Cardinal Bernardin

I entered the seminary when I was only seventeen years old, and ever since then I have been trying to learn how to pray. In those early years, I was under the spiritual care of the **Sulpician** Fathers, both at St. Mary's Seminary in Baltimore and Theological College at Catholic University. They had a special routine that brought us together in the evening to give us points for reflection. In the morning before Mass, we would all gather in what was known as the Prayer Hall to do the reflection. There were times when I wondered whether this was the best form of teaching, but I have to say in retrospect that it certainly introduced me to the importance of prayer and the fact that prayer is not a one-sided practice. Rather, prayer involves speaking and listening on both sides.

After my ordination in 1952, I probably prayed as much as any busy young priest of those days. But in the mid-1970s, I discovered that I was giving a higher priority to good works than to prayer. I was telling others—seminarians, priests, lay people, and religious—about the importance of prayer, emphasizing that they could not really be connected with the Lord unless they prayed. But I felt somewhat hypocritical in my teaching because I was not setting aside adequate time for personal prayer. It was not that I lacked the desire to pray or that I had suddenly decided

Sulpician Relating to the Society of the Priests of Saint Sulpice, a religious order whose ministry is the education of priests.

prayer was not important. Rather, I was very busy, and I fell into the trap of thinking that my good works were more important than prayer.

One evening during this time I spoke to three priests with whom I was having dinner. All three were younger than I, and I had ordained two of them myself since going to Cincinnati [as archbishop] in 1972. During the conversation I told them that

> *If we believe that the Lord Jesus is the Son of God, then of all persons to whom we give of ourselves, we should give him the best we have.*

I was finding it difficult to pray and asked if they could help me. I'm not sure that I was totally honest when I asked for their help because I didn't know whether I would be willing to do what they suggested. "Are you sincere in what you request? Do you really want to turn this around?" they asked. What could I say? I couldn't say no after what I had just told them!

In very direct—even blunt terms—they helped me realize that as a priest and a bishop I was urging a spirituality on others that I was not fully practicing myself. That was a turning point in my life. These priests helped me understand that you have to give what they called, and what many spiritual directors today call, "quality time" to prayer. It can't be done "on the run." You have to put aside good time, quality time. After all, if we believe that the Lord Jesus is the Son of God, then of all persons to whom we give of ourselves, we should give him the best we have.

I decided to give God the first hour of my day, no matter what, to be with him in prayer and meditation where I would try to open the door even wider to his entrance. This put my life in a new and uplifting perspective; I also found that I was able to share the struggles of my own spiritual journey with others. Knowing that I went through the same things they did gave them great encouragement. This has become a crucial element of my ministry with cancer patients and others who are seriously ill.

Still, letting go is never easy. I have prayed and struggled constantly to be able to let go of things more willingly, to be free of everything that keeps the Lord from finding greater hospitality in my soul or interferes with my surrender to what God asks of me.

It is clear that God wants me to let go now. But there is something in us humans that makes us want to hold onto ourselves and everything and everybody familiar to us. My daily prayer is that I can open wide the doors of my heart to Jesus and his expectations of me.

So I now let go more freely, delivered by the Lord from the frustration I sometimes experienced even when I tried before, as earnestly as I could, to break free from the grip of things. I have reflected on Zacchaeus, the tax collector whose story is told in the Gospel of Luke. When he received Jesus into his house, some people complained that Jesus had gone to the home of a sinner. Zacchaeus "stood his ground and said to the Lord, 'I give half my belongings, Lord, to the poor. If I have defrauded anyone in the past, I pay him back fourfold.' And Jesus replied, 'Today salvation has come to this house for this is what it means to be a son of Abraham. The Son of Man has come to search out and save what was lost'" (Cf. Lk 19:1–10).

I have desperately wanted to open the door of my soul as Zacchaeus opened the door of his house. Only in that way can the Lord take over my life completely. Yet many times in the past I have only let him come in part of the way. I talked with him but seemed afraid to let him take over.

Why was I afraid? Why did I open the door only so far and no more? I have searched my soul for answers. At times, I think it was because I wanted to succeed and be acknowledged as a person who has succeeded. At other times I would become upset when I read or heard criticism about my decisions or actions. When these feelings prevailed, I wanted to control things, that is, I wanted to make them come out "right." When I reacted that way, I tended not to put full confidence in people until they had proven themselves to me.

I found that on occasion I have dealt with the Lord in the same way. Conceptually, I understand that he can and should be trusted. I remind myself that it is his Church, that nothing happens beyond his purview. Still, knowing all that, I often found that I would hold back, unwilling to let go completely. . . .

Part of the reason for my reluctance was the fact that every day so many people made demands on me. Their expectations were so numerous, so diverse and personal that I could not seem to free myself as fully as I would have liked from these pressures.

I have also asked whether it was simply pride that haunted me, making me unwilling to take the risk of letting go. Or did I sometimes feel almost paralyzed because I was, in a way, whipsawed by groups in the Church that competed for my attention and support. . . . I felt I had to try in everything to do what is right for the whole Church. Sometimes the resulting tension caused me to be cautious in expressing what I really thought.

To come at this in another way, I wonder if I refused to let the Lord enter all the way into my soul because I feared that he would insist that, in my personal life, I let go of certain things that I was reluctant or unwilling to give up. These were the ordinary things, I knew, and most of them had been gifts from others. Still, I recognized that I could be attached to them.

More than fifteen years ago I gave away all the money I had and said that I would never again have a savings account or stocks. I pledged that I would keep only what was needed to maintain my checking account. I began depositing almost all the monetary gifts in a special account of the Archdiocese that is used for personal charities and special projects of various kinds. Nonetheless, I have received so many gifts in the last few years that I began to save some for myself, using the argument that I might need the funds in retirement or for my aged mother. I have now reexamined all this and ensured that I am free from things so that I am no longer distracted in my relationship with the Lord.

In recent years, as I struggled to let go, I wondered whether God was preparing me for something special—or whether the struggle was only a part of normal spiritual development. It is certainly part of the latter. But now I know that Jesus was preparing me for something special.

The past three years have taught me a great deal about myself and my relationship to God, the Church, and others. Three major events within these years have led me to where I am today. First, the false accusation of sexual misconduct in November 1993 and my eventual reconciliation with my accuser a year later. Second, the diagnosis of pancreatic cancer in June 1995 and the surgery that rendered me "cancer free" for fifteen months. And third, the cancer's return at the end of August 1996, this time in the liver, and my decision to discontinue chemotherapy one month later and live the rest of my life as fully as possible.

Within these major events lies the story of my life—what I have believed and who I have worked hard to be. And because of the nature of these events, I have deepened and developed my own spirituality and gained insights that I want to share. By no means are these reflections meant to be a comprehensive autobiography. They are simply reflections from my heart to yours. I hope they will be of help to you in your own life so you too can enjoy the deep inner peace—God's wonderful gift to me— that I now embrace as I stand on the threshold of eternal life.

For Reflection

1. What do you think Bernardin means when he says that prayer is not a one-sided practice?

2. Based on Bernardin's retelling of the Gospel story of Zacchaeus, what parallels do you see between Zacchaeus and Bernardin? How are their stories different?

3. Bernardin identifies several factors that distracted him from his relationship with God. Choose one and explain in your own words why it might have distracted him. What is distracting you from your own relationship with God?

23 Praying the Psalms

Introduction

Many young people wonder whether the Church is the right place for them—they question some Church teachings or even doubt the truth of the Gospel. In the first reading in this chapter, Kathleen Norris explains that she stopped going to church as a teenager because she thought she had to be a "firm and even cheerful believer" (p. 90). Twenty years later, the Psalms set her straight.

Kathleen Norris is a contemporary poet and author who has written three best-selling memoirs about her spiritual journey. She has served both as a Presbyterian pastor and as a **lay associate** in the **Benedictine** order. Because she drifted away from her childhood faith but continued to look for a spiritual foundation for her life, she can be described as a seeker.

Norris and her husband moved from New York to a South Dakota farm she had inherited. She began attending a tiny Presbyterian church and also visiting a nearby Benedictine monastery. A hallmark of Benedictine spirituality is the Liturgy of the Hours, also known as the Divine Office: the official public, daily prayer of the Church that focuses on the Psalms and is sung at regular hours throughout the day. In this form of communal prayer, Norris says, she discovered that a commitment to praying the Psalms several times a day required her to rethink her concept of worship. She realized that she could

lay associate A person who is not a monk or a nun but who has formally affiliated with a particular monastery. Also known as an oblate.

Benedictine Relating to the religious order founded by Saint Benedict of Nursia in the sixth century, one of the oldest religious orders in the Catholic Church.

pray no matter what her state of mind. The Psalms touched her heart with their powerful poetry even when she was distracted or depressed.

The fact that the Psalms are often angry, even violent, causes us to reflect on the way we too often treat one another, Norris explains in the first reading here. She notes that psalms expressing anguish over God's apparent absence from an unjust world end with a cry for help. Other psalms rejoice in God's just and gracious works. Quoting the poet Emily Dickinson, Norris says that in the psalms, "Pain is indeed 'missed—in Praise,' but in a way that takes pain fully into account" (p. 93). Norris concludes that the Psalms allow both **lamentation** and exultation to be forms of praise, inviting us to bring our true feelings to prayer.

The second reading in this chapter, from Psalm 35, illustrates Norris's observation that psalms sometimes express feelings we might not associate with faith-filled Bible readers—let alone biblical writers. This passage begins with a complaint directed to God: "How long will you look on?" (v. 17). The psalmist describes the evils his enemies are inflicting on him, and he begs God to defend him. But notice the angry tone the psalmist takes: He accuses God of standing by, even of sleeping on the job. Although the psalm expresses frustration at the way the Lord seems to be delaying, it also expresses solid faith in God's power over evil. The psalmist is clearly baffled by God's inaction; but he knows that if and when

lamentation A cry of grief.

God chooses, he will soundly defeat those enemies. The psalmist stands ready to rejoice and praise God, along with all those who support justice, when that day comes.

Excerpt from *The Cloister Walk*
By Kathleen Norris

Not having been to church for some twenty years following high school, I rediscovered the psalms by accident, through my unexpected attraction to Benedictine liturgy, of which the psalms are the mainstay. A Benedictine community recites or sings psalms at morning, noon, and evening prayer, going through the entire **Psalter** every three or four weeks. As I began to immerse myself in monastic liturgy, I found that I was also immersed in poetry and was grateful to find that the poetic nature of the psalms, their constant movement between the mundane and the exalted, means, as British Benedictine Sebastian Moore has said, that "God behaves in the psalms in ways he is not allowed to behave in systematic theology," and also that the images of the psalms, "rough-hewn from earthy experience, [are] absolutely different from formal prayer."

I also discovered, in two nine-month sojourns with the St. John's community, that as Benedictine prayer rolls on, as daily as marriage and washing dishes, it tends to sweep away the concerns of systematic theology and church doctrine. All of that is there, as a kind of scaffolding, but the psalms demand engagement, they ask you to read them with your whole self, praying, as St. Benedict says, "in such a way that our minds are in harmony with our voices." Experiencing the psalms in this way allowed me gradually to let go of that childhood God who had set an impossible standard for both formal prayer and faith, convincing me that religion wasn't worth exploring because I couldn't "do it right."

I learned that when you go to church several times a day, every day, there is no way you can "do it right." You are not always going to sit up straight, let alone think holy thoughts.

Psalter The Book of Psalms of the Old Testament, which contains 150 Psalms.

You're not going to wear your best clothes but whatever isn't in the dirty clothes basket. You come to the Bible's great "book of praises" through all the moods and conditions of life, and while you may feel like hell, you sing anyway. To your surprise, you find that the psalms do not deny your true feelings but allow you to reflect on them, right in front of God and everyone. I soon realized, during my first residency at St. John's, that this is not easy to do on a daily basis. Before, I'd always been a guest in a monastery for a week or less, and the experience was often a high. But now I was in it for a nine-month haul, and it was a struggle for me to go to choir when I didn't feel like it, especially if I was depressed (which, of course, is when I most needed to be there). I took great solace in knowing that everyone there had been through this struggle, and that some of them were struggling now with the absurdity, the monotony of repeating the psalms day after day.

> 66 *To your surprise, you find that the psalms do not deny your true feelings but allow you to reflect on them, right in front of God and everyone.* 99

I found that, even if it took a while—some prayer services I practically slept through, others I seemed to be observing from the planet Mars—the poetry of the psalms would break through and touch me. I became aware of three paradoxes in the psalms: that in them pain is indeed "missed—in Praise," but in a way that takes pain fully into account; that though of all the books of the Bible the psalms speak most directly to the individual, they cannot be removed from a communal context; and that the psalms are holistic in insisting that the mundane and the holy are inextricably linked. The Benedictine method of reading psalms, with long silences between them rather than commentary or explanation, takes full advantage of these paradoxes, offering almost alarming room for interpretation and response. It allows the psalms their full poetic power, their use of imagery and hyperbole ("Awake, my soul, / awake lyre and harp, / I will awake the dawn" [Ps. 57:8]), repetition and contradiction, as tools of word-play as well as the play of human emotions. For all of their discipline, the Benedictines allowed me to relax and sing again in church; they allowed me, as one older sister, a widow with ten children, described it, to "let the words of the psalms wash over me, and experience the joy of just being with words." As a poet I like to be with words. It was a revelation to me that this could be prayer; that this could be enough.

But to the modern reader the psalms can seem impenetrable: how in the world can we read, let alone pray, these angry and often violent poems from an ancient warrior culture? At a glance they seem overwhelmingly patriarchal, ill-tempered, moralistic, vengeful, and often seem to reflect precisely what is wrong with our world. And that's the point, or part of it. As one reads the psalms every day, it becomes clear that the world they depict is not really so different from our own; the fourth-century monk Athanasius wrote that the psalms "become like a mirror to the person singing them," and this is as true now as when he wrote it. The psalms remind us that the way we judge each other, with harsh words and acts of vengeance, constitutes injustice, and they remind us that it is the powerless in society who are overwhelmed when injustice becomes institutionalized. Psalm 35, like many psalms, laments God's absence in our unjust world, even to the point of crying. "How long, O Lord, will you look on?" (v. 17). I take an odd comfort in recognizing that the ending of Psalm 12 is as relevant now as when it was written thousands of years ago: "Protect us forever from this generation / [for] . . . the worthless are praised to the skies" (vv. 7–8).

But this is not comfortable reading, and it goes against the American grain. A writer, whose name I have forgotten, once said that the true religions of America are optimism and denial. The psalms demand that we recognize that praise does not spring from a delusion that things are better than they are, but rather from the human capacity for joy. Only when we see this can we understand that both lamentation ("Out of the depths I cry to you, O Lord" [Ps. 130:1]) and exultation ("Cry with joy to the Lord, all the earth" [Ps. 100:1]) can be forms of praise. In our skeptical age, which favors appraisal over praise, the psalms are evidence that praise need not be a fruit of optimism.

Psalm 35:17–28

O Lord, how long will you look on?
> Restore my soul from their destruction,
> my very life from lions!
Then I will thank you in the great assembly;
> I will praise you before the mighty throng.
Do not let lying foes rejoice over me,
> my undeserved enemies wink knowingly.
They speak no words of peace,
> but against the quiet in the land
> they fashion deceitful speech.
They open wide their mouths against me.
> They say, "Aha! Good!
> Our eyes have seen it!"
You see this, LORD; do not be silent;
> Lord, do not withdraw from me.
Awake, be vigilant in my defense,
> in my cause, my God and my Lord.
Defend me because you are just, LORD;
> my God, do not let them rejoice over me.
Do not let them say in their hearts,
> "Aha! Our soul!"
Do not let them say,
> "We have devoured that one!"
Put to shame and confound
> all who relish my misfortune.
Clothe with shame and disgrace
> those who lord it over me.
But let those who favor my just cause
> shout for joy and be glad.
May they ever say, "Exalted be the LORD
> who delights in the peace of his loyal servant."
Then my tongue shall recount your justice,
> declare your praise, all the day long.

For Reflection

1. Norris says that the Psalms "demand engagement." What do you think she means?

2. How does Norris find meaning in the Psalms even though, as she says, they are the product of an "ancient warrior culture"?

3. Norris concludes that praise need not always spring from optimism. What does she mean? How is it possible to praise God even when we are not feeling optimistic about the world?

4. Psalm 35 mentions "lying foes" and "undeserved enemies." What enemies of just causes might modern believers ask God to defeat?

24 The Prayer Jesus Taught Us

Introduction

How fast can you recite the Lord's Prayer? In eight seconds? six seconds? Here is a harder question: How slowly can you pray it? Because we have prayed this prayer so many times, we can rush through reciting it without giving any thought to its meaning. It can be a remarkable experience to reflect prayerfully on each sentence, each line, each phrase.

The *Catechism of the Catholic Church* includes a substantial discussion of the Lord's Prayer, because its words are not only a prayer but also a summary of all that we believe as Christians. In a brief excerpt in this chapter, the *Catechism* points out that Jesus can teach us to pray in a way that no one else ever could. Why? Because Jesus is not just a great teacher. He is the Eternal Word of God, one of the Persons of the Holy Trinity. Jesus is able to offer us words the Father would have us pray. But Jesus is also the Eternal Word Incarnate; he is a human being who completely understands our needs. So in addition to giving us the words that express our deepest longings, he sent us the Holy Spirit, who makes the words come alive in our hearts.

The second reading in this chapter is a selection from *Our Father*, a book by Fr. Bernard Häring that presents an in-depth meditation on the Lord's Prayer. Many consider Häring to be the most important moral theologian of the twentieth century, because of his influence on the teachings of the Second Vatican Council. He emphasized a theology of love at a time when most discussions of morality were limited to a focus on sin.

In this reading from *Our Father*, Häring writes about what happens when we enter into the Lord's Prayer with our whole hearts.

Then he turns to Baptism: Jesus' Baptism and our own. At first it may seem strange that Häring connects the Our Father to Jesus' Baptism. But recall that in the Gospel narratives of this event, God calls Jesus "Son"; and in the prayer Jesus taught us, he calls God "Father." From there it is a small step to the idea that our own Baptism unites us to the Son, so that we too can call God "Father."

Häring also explores the life that a wholehearted commitment to the Our Father calls us to lead—a life that honors the twofold commandment to love God and neighbor. Häring is referring to the Gospel story in which someone (most likely an adversary trying to stump him) asked Jesus to name the greatest commandment. In reply Jesus drew on Scripture, summarizing a passage from Deuteronomy: "You shall love the Lord, your God, with all your heart, with all your soul, and with all your mind. This is the greatest and the first commandment. The second is like it: You shall love your neighbor as yourself" (Matthew 22:37–39). Häring suggests that the Our Father is all about living that "double commandment" (p. 17).

Both readings in this chapter call us to do more than just recite the Our Father. They call us to enter into the prayer Jesus taught us and, through it, to enter into God's plan for us and for the world.

The Baptism of Jesus

The Gospels of Matthew, Mark, and Luke each include an account of Jesus' Baptism in the Jordan River by Saint John the Baptist. As Jesus emerges from the water, two things happen. The Holy Spirit, in the form of a dove, descends from the heavens to anoint Jesus for his ministry, just as the Spirit anointed prophets and kings in the Old Testament. Then something even more surprising happens: A voice from Heaven proclaims Jesus to be the beloved Son of God.

Excerpt from the *Catechism of the Catholic Church*

2765. The traditional expression "the Lord's Prayer"—*oratio Dominica*—means that the prayer to our Father is taught and given to us by the Lord Jesus. The prayer that comes to us from Jesus is truly unique: it is "of the Lord." On the one hand, in the words of this prayer the only Son gives us the words the Father gave him:[1] he is the master of our prayer. On the other, as Word incarnate, he knows in his human heart the needs of his human brothers and sisters and reveals them to us: he is the model of our prayer.

2766. But Jesus does not give us a formula to repeat mechanically.[2] As in every vocal prayer, it is through the Word of God that the Holy Spirit teaches the children of God to pray to their Father. Jesus not only gives us the words of our **filial** prayer; at the same time he gives us the Spirit by whom these words become in us "spirit and life."[3] Even more, the proof and possibility of our filial prayer is that the Father "sent the Spirit of his Son into our hearts, crying, '***Abba***! Father!'"[4] Since our prayer sets forth our desires before God, it is again the Father, "he who searches the hearts of men," who "knows what is the mind of the Spirit, because the Spirit intercedes for the saints according to the will of God."[5] The prayer to Our Father is inserted into the mysterious mission of the Son and of the Spirit.

filial Appropriate for a son or daughter.

Abba Aramaic for "my Father" or "our Father." A way of addressing God the Father, used by Jesus to call attention to his—and our—intimate relationship with his Heavenly Father.

Endnotes

1. Cf. *John* 17:7.
2. Cf. *Matthew* 6:7; *1 Kings* 18:26-29.
3. *John* 6:63.
4. *Galatians* 4:6.
5. *Romans* 8:27.

Excerpt from *Our Father*

By Bernard Häring

Profession of Faith as Worship and Praise

The *Our Father* is a condensed profession of faith, which Jesus lived out and which instructs us. Only in worship and praise can we acknowledge faith in God, who is love in person. It is at the same time a commitment to acknowledge, honour and glorify God, who has revealed himself as love in the whole of our lives, above all in the realisation of his loving, caring, healing and forgiving love for all humanity.

Faith in the fullest sense is not just saying and expressing all that we hold to be true. Faith means, more ultimately, securing oneself in God, to love and honour him in thought, word and deed as our one and all.

When we pray the *Our Father* with our whole hearts, faith and life, religion and morality become an inseparable synthesis. In the communion of saints, united with Jesus, we commit ourselves—always trusting

> *When we pray the* **Our Father** *with our whole hearts, faith and life, religion and morality become an inseparable synthesis.*

God's grace—to root our faith so deeply in our hearts, that he can shape all our senses and endeavours and also our action.

The *Our Father* Is Trinitarian

Our prayer is always connected to our baptism. This in turn must be understood in the light of Jesus' baptism. Jesus' baptism in the Jordan forms a whole with the baptism of Jesus in the Holy Spirit and in his blood.

Jesus sees the descent of the Holy Spirit in the form of a dove of peace. He knows that the Father has named him the beloved Son, on whom all his favour rests. In everything he says, proclaims and does, his is filled with the consciousness that "the Spirit of the Lord rests on me, he has anointed me" (*Luke 4:16*). In the Holy Spirit, in the breath of the love of the Father he rejoices "Abba, Father" (*Luke 10:21*). In the power of the Holy Spirit he consecrates himself and is consecrated by the Father for the salvation of the world.

When we make the sign of the cross or pray the *Our Father*, we do it in the light of Jesus' baptism and our communion with Jesus by the power of our baptism in the name of the triune God. We dare to use the unprecedented, bold address "Abba, Abbuni," "Father, our Father," because we know we are united with Jesus, gifted and sanctified through his Spirit.

The *Our Father* only really becomes the basic form of our faith and [at] the same time our whole life's programme insofar as we consciously, gratefully and trustingly are aware of the trinitarian dimension of our Christian being, our faith and prayer.

Only in union with Jesus and animated and graced by his Holy Spirit do we enter into prayer and live before the countenance of Jesus' Abba, our Abba.

The trinitarian dimension of our prayer makes it an event that already contains a foretaste of heaven.

The Whole of Our Life's Programme

The whole of our life's programme and our call are contained in this double commandment: to love God with our whole heart and, united with Jesus and the Father in the power of the divine breath of love, to love our neighbour, not least the poor.

The first part of the *Our Father*, "Hallowed be Thy name," is summed up in the bold, loving "Thou"[1] we address to God, who has revealed himself to us as love. It is a joyful "thank you" to be allowed to address, love and praise the Almighty intimately as our Father, as "Thou."

It is the vow to test all our reflection, striving and action by whether and how seriously we take the name of the Father and our call as his sons and daughters, and honour it. Not least, we are confronted here above all with our mission to honour the one God and Father, to further peace and the solidarity of salvation for all people.

Careful reflection on Jesus' preaching of the Kingdom of God makes the love and worship of the Father concrete. Day by day, challenges and opportunities present themselves to testify to the Kingdom of God as the Kingdom of love and justice, of humility and reconciliation. How do we make it evident to people that our thinking, speaking, action are all about the Kingdom of love of God and neighbour which Christ proclaimed and made visible? God revealed his inexhaustible, glorious plan of salvation (his will) to us in his beloved Son.

We cannot pray for his will to be done day by day without constantly trying to meditate on and discover God's plan of salvation in the signs of the times. In doing so we are continually examining how seriously we take God's plan of salvation, seeking to understand it and acknowledging it in practice. It is an essential feature of our self-commitment, made in the power of the Holy Spirit, and always in the light of the beloved Son, to love God in all and above all and to fulfil his holy will of love.

The second part of the *Our Father* is about loving your neighbour along with Jesus. It is about us, the radical common life of Jesus' solidarity of salvation with all people in all spheres of life.

Just as the baptism of Jesus in the river Jordan was a trinitarian event, praying the *Our Father* takes us into the trinitarian life of God. Keeping this in mind, together with our fundamental option for the solidarity of salvation in all aspects of life, will doubtless help us to make our life's programme clearer and clearer, with more convincing contours.

Endnote

1. Translator's note: in German, as in the English of the past, "thou" and not "you" is the intimate address reserved for those to whom we are particularly close.

For Reflection

1. The first reading, from the *Catechism*, tells us that the Holy Spirit ensures that that the words of the Our Father become "spirit and life" in us. Explain this idea further in your own words.

2. In the second excerpt, Häring says that the Lord's Prayer is a profession of faith, or a creed. What beliefs do you see reflected in this prayer?

3. Based on both readings, how is each person of the Trinity involved when we call God "Father"?

4. What does praying for God's Kingdom demand of us, according to Häring?

For Further Reading

Benedict. *Many Religions, One Covenant: Israel, the Church, and the World.* San Francisco: Ignatius Press, 1999.

Bernardin, Joseph. *The Gift of Peace: Personal Reflections.* New York: Image Books, 1997.

Dogmatic Constitution on the Church (Lumen Gentium). Second Vatican Council, 1964.

Dogmatic Constitution on Divine Revelation (Dei Verbum). Second Vatican Council, 1965.

Häring, Bernard. *Our Father.* British-American ed. Winona, MN: Saint Mary's Press, 1996.

John Paul II, Pope and Saint, with Vittorio Messori. *Crossing the Threshold of Hope.* New York: Knopf, 1994.

Karris, Robert J., and Dianne Bergant. *The Collegeville Bible Commentary: Based on the New American Bible.* Collegeville, MN: Liturgical Press, 1992.

Lewis, C. S. *Christian Behaviour: A Further Series of Broadcast Talks.* New York: Macmillan, 1944.

McKenna, Megan. *Parables: The Arrows of God.* Maryknoll, NY: Orbis Books, 1994.

Mitchell, Patricia, ed. *Wisdom of the Fathers.* Touching the Risen Christ series. Ijamsville, MD: Word Among Us Press, 1999.

Mother Teresa. *In the Heart of the World: Thoughts, Stories, and Prayers.* Novato, CA: New World Library, 1997.

Pennington, M. Basil. *Challenges in Prayer: A Classic with a New Introduction.* Rev. ed. Liguori, MO: Liguori Publications, 2005.

Rupp, Joyce. *May I Have This Dance?* Notre Dame, IN: Ave Maria Press, 1992.

Sheen, Fulton J. *The Eternal Galilean.* Garden City, NY: Garden City Publishing, 1937.

Shepherd, Jerry. *Teens and Spirituality.* Being Real series. Winona, MN: Saint Mary's Press, 2005.

Acknowledgments

The excerpts labeled *Catechism* and *CCC* are from the English translation of the *Catechism of the Catholic Church* for use in the United States of America, second edition. Copyright © 1994 by the United States Catholic Conference, Inc.—Libreria Editrice Vaticana (LEV). English translation of the *Catechism of the Catholic Church: Modifications from the Editio Typica* copyright © 1997 by the United States Catholic Conference, Inc.—LEV.

The excerpt on pages 12–15 and the quotations on page 15, and in reflection questions 1 and 4 on page 16, and the excerpt on pages 12–15 are from *The Collegeville Bible Commentary*, Dianne Bergant and Robert J. Karris, general editors (Collegeville, MN: Liturgical Press, 1989), pages 16, 16, 17, and 16–17, respectively. Copyright © 1992 by the Order of St. Benedict, Collegeville, MN. Used with permission of Liturgical Press.

The quotation on page 17 is from the transcript of an interview with George Coyne on the PBS documentary *Faith and Reason*, at *www.pbs.org/faithandreason/transcript/coyne-frame.html*.

The first two quotations on page 18 are from Pope Saint John Paul II's "Message to the Pontifical Academy of Sciences: On Evolution," numbers 2 and 3, at *www.ewtn.com/library/papaldoc/jp961022.htm*. Copyright © LEV.

The third quotation on page 18 is from "Encyclical *Humani Generis* of the Holy Father Pius XIII," number 36, at *www.vatican.va/holy_father/pius_xii/encyclicals/documents/hf_p-xii_enc_12081950_humani-generis_en.html*. Copyright © LEV.

The last quotation on page 18 is from "The Vatican Claims Darwin's Theory of Evolution is Compatible with Christianity," by Chris Irvine, in

year 1, by the USCCB (Collegeville, MN: Liturgical Press, 2002), page 91. Copyright © 2001, 1998, 1992, 1986 Confraternity of Christian Doctrine (CCD), Washington, D.C. Used with permission of the CCD, Washington, D.C. No portion of this text may be reproduced by any means without permission in writing from the copyright owner.

The excerpt on pages 57–59 is from *The Ante-Nicene Fathers*, edited by Alexander Roberts and James Donaldson (n.p.: Christian Literature Publishing Company, 1885–1896).

The excerpt on pages 59–61 is from the English translation of *The Liturgy of the Hours*, copyright © 1970, 1973, 1975, International Commission on English in the Liturgy Corporation (ICEL) (New York: Catholic Book Publishing, 1975), volume I, pages 446–448. Illustrations and arrangement copyright © 1975 by Catholic Book Publishing Company, New York. Used with permission of the ICEL.

The quotations on pages 63, 64, and in reflection question 3 on page 68, and the excerpt on pages 64–67 are from "Jesus Reveals the Father," an interview with Fr. Marie-Dominique Philippe, OP, at *www.stjean.com/EN/Letter_29.htm*. Copyright © Congregation of St. John. Used with permission of the Congregation of St. John.

The excerpt on pages 73–75 is from *The Gospel of Matthew*, by Daniel J. Harrington (Collegeville, MN: Liturgical Press, 1991), pages 68–70. Copyright © 1991 by the Order of St. Benedict, Collegeville, MN. Used with permission of Liturgical Press.

The excerpt on pages 79–83 and the quotation in reflection question 4 on page 83 are from *Parables: The Arrows of God*, by Megan McKenna (Maryknoll, NY: Orbis Books, 1994), pages 26–29. Copyright © 1994 by Megan McKenna. Used with permission of Orbis Books.

The excerpt on pages 86–89 and the quotation in reflection question 1 on page 90 are from *The Miracles of Jesus and the Theology of Miracles*, by René Latourelle, translated by Matthew J. O'Connell (New York, Mahwah, NJ: Paulist Press, 1988), pages 282–284. Copyright © Les Éditions Bellarmin, Montreal, originally published as *Miracles de Jésus et théologie du miracle*. English translation copyright © 1988 by The Missionary Society of St. Paul the Apostle in the State of New York. Used with permission.

The words from the Mass on page 91 are from the English translation of *The Roman Missal* © 2010, ICEL. All rights reserved. Used with permission of the ICEL.

The excerpts on pages 92–95 and the quotation in reflection question 1 on page 96 are from *Meditations by John Baptist de La Salle*, translated by Richard Arnandez and Augustine Loes, edited by Augustine Loes and Francis Huether (Landover, MD: Lasallian Publications, 1994), pages 114–117. Copyright © 1994 by Christian Brothers Conference. All rights reserved. Used with permission of the Christian Brothers Conference.

The quotations on page 100 and in reflection question 4 on page 104, and the excerpt on pages 103–104 are from *God's Mercy Endures Forever: Guidelines on the Presentation of Jews and Judaism in Catholic Preaching*, numbers 22, 7, and 22, respectively, by the USCCB, at *old.usccb.org/liturgy/godsmercy.shtml*. Copyright © 2008 USCCB. All rights reserved. Used with permission of the USCCB.

The excerpt on pages 101–103 and the quotation in reflection question 3 on page 104 are from *Declaration on the Relation of the Church to Non-Christian Religions* (*Nostra Aetate*, 1965), number 4, at *www.vatican.va/archive/hist_councils/ii_vatican_council/documents/vat-ii_decl_19651028_nostra-aetate_en.html*. Copyright © LEV. Used with permission of LEV.

The excerpt on pages 106–109 and the quotation in the sidebar on page 108 are from *The Eternal Galilean*, by Fulton J. Sheen (Garden City, NY: Garden City Publishing Company, 1950), pages 269–274. Copyright © 1934 by D. Appleton-Century Company. Used with permission of the Society for the Propagation of the Faith.

The quotations on pages 110 and 111 and the excerpts on pages 112–113 and 114–115 are from the English translation of *The Liturgy of the Hours*, copyright © 1970, 1973, 1975, ICEL (New York: Catholic Book Publishing Company, 1976), volume II, pages 816, 816–817, 898, 815–817, and 898–899, respectively. Illustrations and arrangement copyright © 1975 by Catholic Book Publishing Company, New York. Used with permission of the ICEL.

The excerpt on pages 118–122 is from *May I Have This Dance?* by Joyce Rupp (Notre Dame, IN: Ave Maria Press, 1992), pages 70–74.

The quotation on page 124 and the excerpt on pages 125–129 are from "When Death Will Not Leave: A Husband's Journey Through Grief," by James R. Kelly, in *America*, April 14, 2008, at *www. americamagazine.org/content/article.cfm?article_id=10738.* Copyright © America Press, 2008. Used with permission of America Press.

The quotations on page 131 and in reflection question 3 on page 136, and the excerpt on pages 133–135 are from *Crossing the Threshold of Hope*, by His Holiness John Paul II, edited by Vittorio Messori (New York: Alfred A. Knopf, 1994), pages 222, 218, 218–219, and 222–224, respectively. Copyright © 1994 by Arnoldo Mondadori Editore. Translation copyright © 1994 by Alfred A. Knopf. Used with permission of Alfred A. Knopf, a division of Random House, Inc.

The excerpt on pages 132–133 and the quotation in reflection question 2 on page 136 are from *Dogmatic Constitution on the Church (Lumen Gentium*, 1964), numbers 40–41 and 40, at *www.vatican.va/archive/ hist_councils/ii_vatican_council/documents/vat-ii_const_19641121_lumen-gentium_en.html.* Copyright © LEV. Used with permission of LEV.

The quotation on page 138 and the excerpt on pages 138–141 are from *Christian Behaviour*, by C. S. Lewis (New York: Macmillan, 1944), pages 62 and 59–62. Copyright © 1943 by the Macmillan Company. Used with permission of the C. S. Lewis Company Ltd.

The quotations on pages 142, 143, and in reflection question 2 on page 147, and the excerpt on pages 143–145 are from *Teens and Spirituality*, by Jerry Shepherd (Winona, MN: Saint Mary's Press, 2005), pages 31, 31, 32, and 31–32, respectively. Copyright © 2005 by Jerry Shepherd. Originally published by Little Hills Press Pty Ltd., Sydney, Australia.

The second quotation on page 142 and the excerpt on pages 145–147 are from "Living the Sacramental Life: Teaching Our Youth by Example," by Anna Nicole Kyritsis, in *Praxis*, volume 3, July 2002. Copyright © 2002, Department of Religious Education of the Greek Orthodox Archdiocese of America. Used with permission of the Greek Orthodox Archdiocese of America.

The excerpt on pages 152–154 and the quotation in reflection question 3 on page 155 are from *Challenges in Prayer: A Classic with a New Introduction*, by M. Basil Pennington (Liguori, MO: Liguori Publications, 2005), pages 5–8, 10, and 8, respectively. Copyright © 1982 by Michael Glazier; copyright © 2005 by Cistercian Abbey of Spencer. Used with permission of Liguori Press.

The quotation on page 150 is from the Saint Joseph's Abbey Web site, at *www.spencerabbey.org/begin.html.*

The quotations on pages 156 and 157 and the excerpt on pages 158–162 are from *The Gift of Peace: Personal Reflections*, by Joseph Cardinal Bernardin (Chicago: Loyola Press, 1997), pages 4, 4, 6, ix, x, and 4–11, respectively. Copyright © 1997 Catholic Bishop of Chicago, a Corporation Sole. Used with permission of Loyola Press. To order copies call 1-800-621-1008 or go to *www.loyolapress.com.*

The quotations on pages 163 and 164 and in reflection questions 1 and 2 on page 169, and the excerpt on pages 165–167 are from *The Cloister Walk*, by Kathleen Norris (New York: Berkley Publishing Group, 1996], pages 90, 93, and 91–94, respectively. Copyright © 1996 by Kathleen Norris. Used with permission of Riverhead Books, an imprint of Penguin Group (USA), Inc. Grail Psalms © 1963, 1986 by Ladies of The Grail, England. Used with permission of GIA, Inc.

The quotation on page 171 and the excerpt on pages 173–175 are from *Our Father*, by Bernard Häring, translation by Gwen Griffith-Dickson (Winona, MN: Saint Mary's Press, 1996), pages 17 and 15–18. Copyright © 1995 by Bernard Häring. Used with permission of the Congregation of the Most Holy Redeemer, Province of Munich.

To view copyright terms and conditions for Internet materials cited here, log on to the home pages for the referenced Web sites.

During this book's preparation, all citations, facts, figures, names, addresses, telephone numbers, Internet URLs, and other pieces of information cited within were verified for accuracy. The authors and Saint Mary's Press staff have made every attempt to reference current and valid sources, but we cannot guarantee the content of any source, and we are not responsible for any changes that may have occurred since our verification. If you find an error in, or have a question or concern about, any of the information or sources listed within, please contact Saint Mary's Press.

Endnotes Cited in Quotations from the *Catechism of the Catholic Church,* Second Edition

Chapter 17

1. *1 Corinthians* 2:9.

Chapter 24

1. *John* 6:63.